ONE-HOUR
Cross Stitch

One-Hour Cross Stitch

©1992 by Oxmoor House, Inc.
Book Division of Southern Progress Corporation
P.O. Box 2463
Birmingham, Alabama 35201

Library of Congress Catalog Card Number: 92-060991
ISBN: 0-8487-1097-5
Manufactured in the United States of America
First Printing 1992

Editor-in-Chief: Nancy J. Fitzpatrick
Senior Editor: Mary Kay Culpepper
Editor: Cecilia C. Robinson
Director of Manufacturing: Jerry Higdon
Production Manager: Rick Litton
Associate Production Manager: Theresa L. Beste
Production Assistant: Pam Beasley Bullock

Symbol of Excellence Publishers, Inc., Staff

Editors: Barbara Cockerham, Phyllis Hoffman
Associate Editor: Diane Kennedy-Jackson
Copy Editor: Lorna Reeves
Production Manager: Wayne Hoffman
Creative Director: Mac Jamieson
Art Director: Yukie McLean
Associate Production Manager: Perry James
Editorial Assistants: Cindy Housel, Carol Odom
Staff Artists: Charles Long, Michael Whisenant
Photography Stylists: Ashley Cobb, Charlotte Holder, Ada Parker, Tracey M. Runnion, Claudia Wood

Introduction

How many cross stitches can be formed in an hour? That thought-provoking question led to this book filled with great designs that can be accomplished in approximately 60 minutes.

How many cross stitches can be formed in an hour? A test among our stitchers indicated that approximately 150 stitches with two color changes can be made in one hour. With that in mind, our designers went to work to create the collection of wonderful, quick-stitch designs presented throughout these pages! We're not saying that every design included has exactly 150 stitches with two color changes. Some are comprised of a few less or a few more stitches, some require several floss colors, and a few go beyond our guidelines. But we just had to share them with you!

To keep the finishing time as well as the stitching time minimal, we worked most of our designers' creations on pre-finished pieces made especially for cross stitch. Waste canvas and linen used as waste canvas on an assortment of ready-made garments and household items purchased at local discount stores made stitching fun and finishing easy. *See instructions on pages 140 and 141.*

The designs include an array of motifs, from tiny stitched houses to miniature Christmas-inspired creations. Most of the designs are very versatile; we've chosen several of them and stitched them on a variety of items, including useful, decorative table linens and wearing apparel with eye-catching appeal!

Within these pages, you'll find over 180 designs, each requiring about an hour to stitch and used in varying combinations to make more than 170 projects. Choose your favorite designs and work them on purchased pieces or on treasures long-since forgotten in your closets and chest of drawers. Use our ideas to inspire your creativity. Then use your skills with needle and floss to work your favorite stitchery on pieces you'll enjoy day after day.

Contents

For Grown-ups

Transform purchased garments into one-of-a-kind wearables with needle, floss, and this collection of great designs. From nautical-inspired sea dwellers to delicate flowers to watermelons with a taste of whimsy, you'll find wonderful motifs for adorning your favorite fashions in style.

Buttons, Buttons, Buttons

Button covers make changing the look of a blouse or jacket as easy as 1-2-3! Cross stitch placed on ready-to-cover button covers gives you the option of varying the look of a single piece of clothing to fit a variety of occasions or giving a brand-new look to an old favorite. Follow manufacturer's directions for finishing and enjoy these no-sewing-required "fasteners." To finish, glue the covered piece to a purchased button-cover snap and slide your assembled button cover over the existing button on the garment. Charts begin on page 10.

FARM ANIMALS

	DMC	COLOR
•	310	black
o	white	white
ϕ	606	orange-red
W	318	steel gray, lt.
P	754	peach flesh, lt.
ↄ	742	tangerine, lt.
3	744	yellow, pl.
Z	699	green
X	740	tangerine

Fabric: 18-count ivory Ainring from Zweigart®

Stitch count:

Pig	10H x 22W
Duck	14H x 21W
Sheep	13H x 23W
Rooster	19H x 20W
Cow	14H x 24W

Design size:

Pig	18-count	⅝" x 1¼"
Duck	18-count	¾" x 1¼"
Sheep	18-count	¾" x 1¼"
Rooster	18-count	1" x 1⅛"
Cow	18-count	¾" x 1⅜"

Instructions: Cross stitch using two strands of floss. Backstitch using one strand of floss. Make French knots where • appears at intersecting grid lines using two strands of floss, wrapping floss around needle once. Make straight stitches for grass blades using one strand 699.

Backstitch instructions:

742	chick's beak and foot
310	pig's tail

French knot instructions:

318	sheep's eyes
310	remainder of eyes
white	pig's nostrils

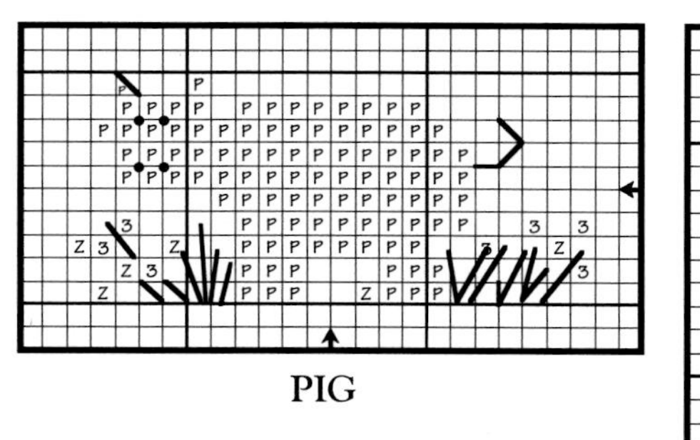

PIG

DUCK

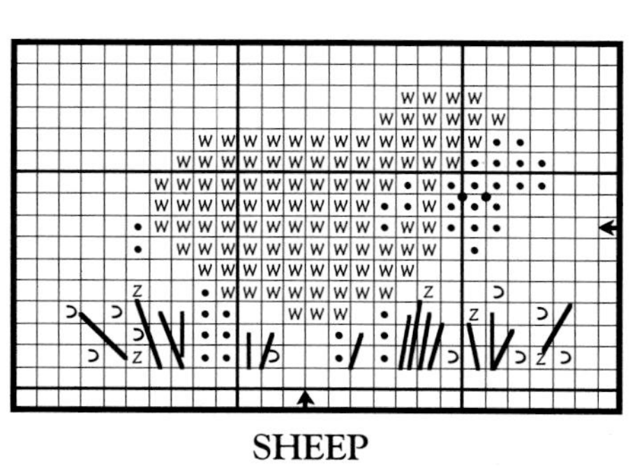

SHEEP

ROOSTER

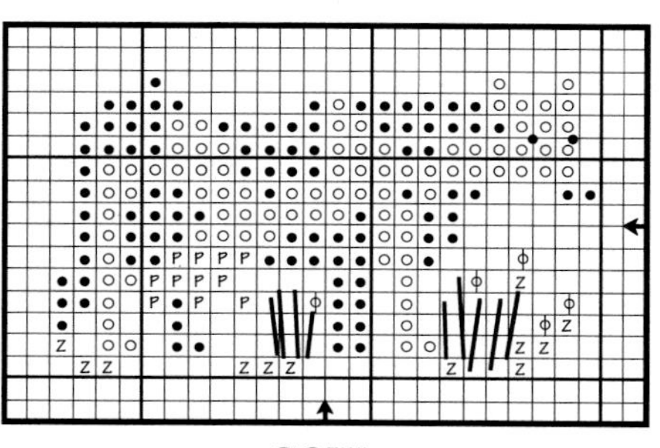

COW

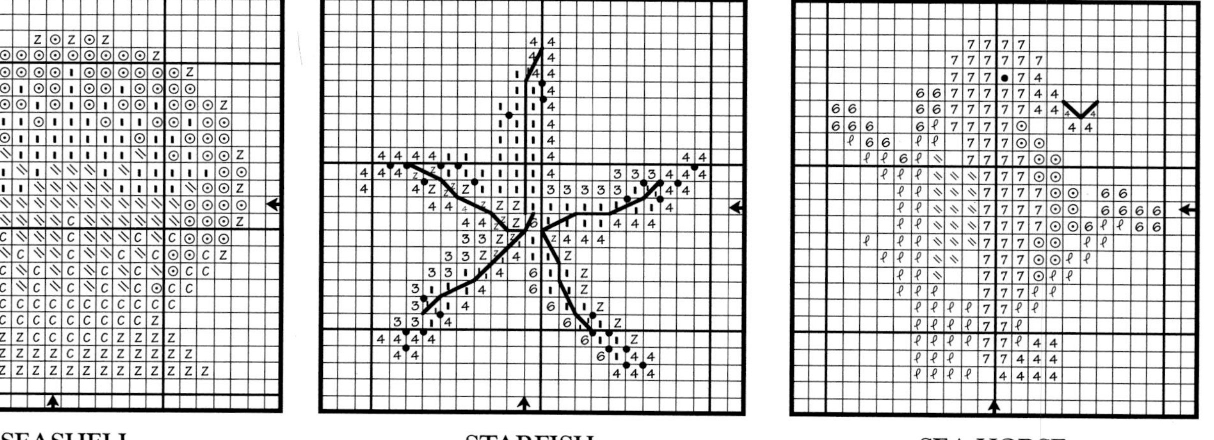

SEASHELL

STARFISH

SEA HORSE

CIRCUS CLOWNS

	DMC	COLOR
O	699	green
6	604	cranberry, lt.
#	3021	brown-gray, dk.
B	798	delft, dk.
S	744	yellow, pl.
\\	3746	blue-violet, dk.
Δ	601	cranberry, dk.
ℓ	3340	apricot, med.
I	945	flesh
•	310	black

Fabric: 18-count ivory Ainring from Zweigart®
Stitch count: 20H x 20W
Design size:
18-count 1⅛" x 1⅛"

Instructions: Cross stitch using two strands of floss. Backstitch using one strand of floss. Make French knots where • appears at intersecting grid lines using two strands of floss, wrapping floss around needle once.
Backstitch instructions:
604 mouths
310 eyebrows, balloon strings

French knot instructions:
310 eyes
798 buttons

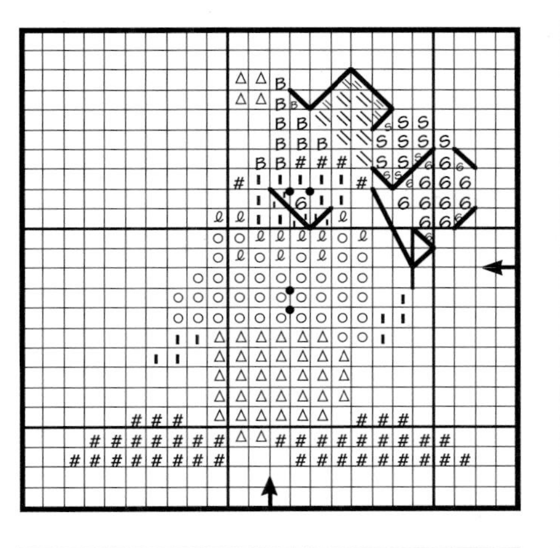

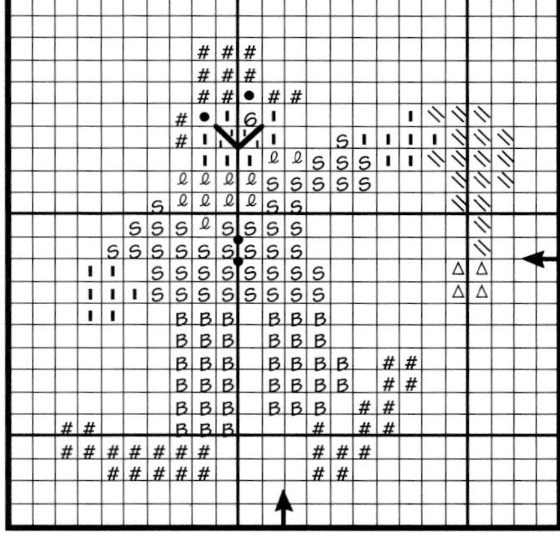

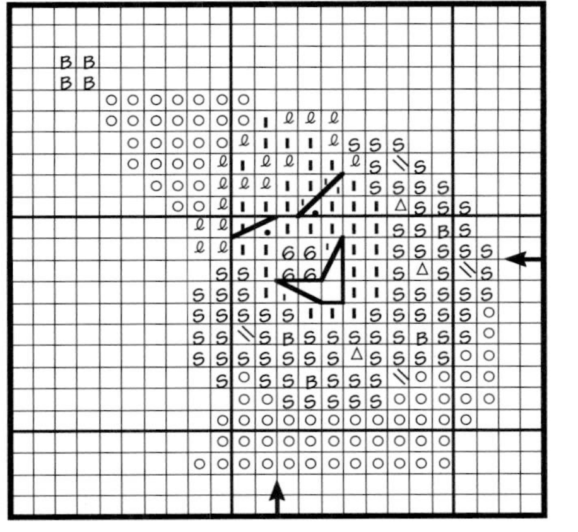

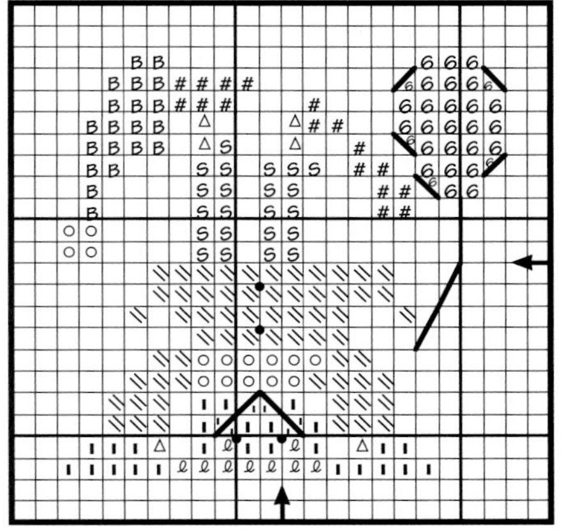

SEA LIFE

	DMC	COLOR
⊙	819	baby pink, lt.
\\	353	peach flesh
C	352	coral, lt.
Z	3727	mauve, lt.
I	745	yellow, lt. pl.
7	407	flesh, dk.
4	3046	yellow-beige, med.
3	964	sea green, lt.
6	932	antique blue, lt.
ℓ [	964	sea green, lt.
	932	antique blue, lt.
•	310	black

Fabrics: ***Button Covers***—18-count ivory Ainring from Zweigart®; ***Tote Bag***—28-count linen used as waste canvas
Stitch count: 21H x 21W

Design size:

Button Covers	18-count	1⅛" x 1⅛"
Tote Bag	28-count	1½" x 1½"

Button Covers (Photo is on page 8.)
Instructions: Cross stitch using two strands of floss. Backstitch using one strand 3046. Make French knots where • appears at intersecting grid lines using two strands 407, wrapping floss around needle once. When two colors are bracketed together, use one strand of each.

Tote Bag (Photo is on page 30.)
Instructions: Cross stitch over two threads using two strands of floss. Backstitch using one strand 3046. Make French knots where • appears at intersecting grid lines using two strands 407, wrapping floss around needle once. When two colors are bracketed together, use one strand of each. Stitch *Angelfish* 2" down from top of tote bag and ¾" in from left side of center panel. Stitch *Starfish* 2" down from top of tote bag and ¾" in from right side of center panel. Stitch *Sea Horse* 5" down from top of tote bag and ¾" in from left side of center panel. Stitch *Striped Fish* 5" down from top of tote bag and ¾" in from right side of center panel.

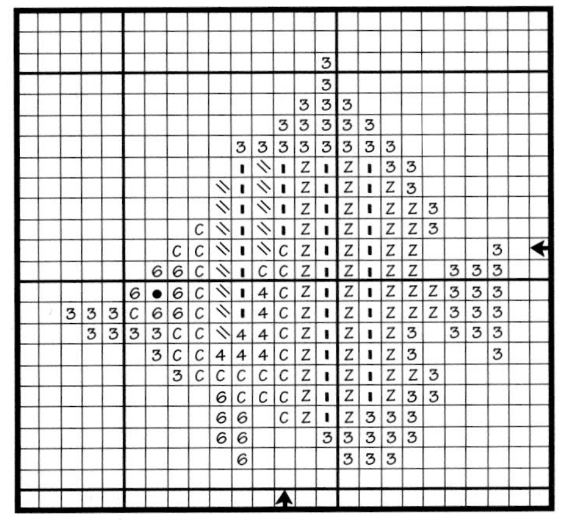

STRIPED FISH

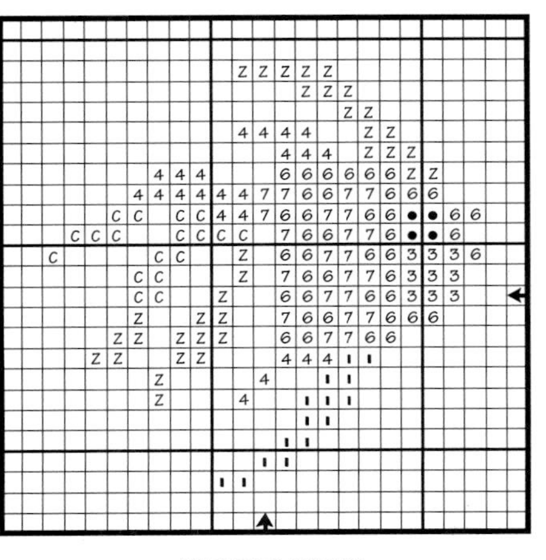

ANGELFISH

Watermelons

Watermelon, the succulent fruit we enjoy throughout the summer, is a favorite for many. Ply the stitches to create this progressive feast along the Aida insert of a comfy sweatshirt, or choose a single motif from the chart and stitch it atop a blouse pocket, on a shirt collar, or anywhere, using waste canvas or linen. Chart is on page 14.

School Days

School supplies are put to new uses when produced with needle and floss! These quick-stitch reminders of those "golden rule days" are ideal for adding to blouses, totes, book bags, and cloth lunch sacks. Worked together on a polo shirt, they'll make a fast-to-finish gift for a special teacher. Chart is on page 14.

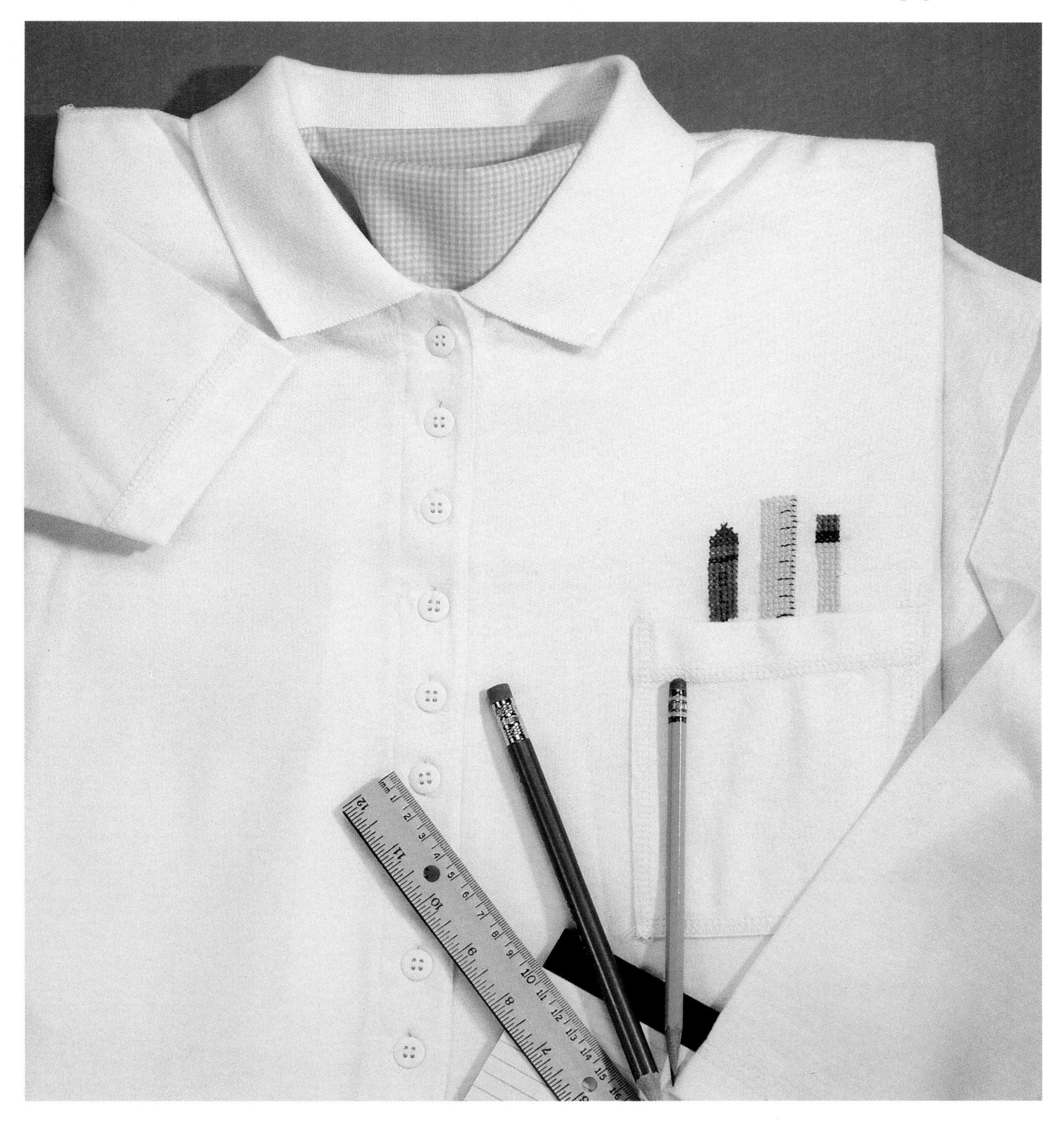

SCHOOL DAYS

	DMC	COLOR
–	743	yellow, med.
Z	797	royal blue
X	826	blue, med.
//	320	pistachio, med.
ℓ	817	coral red, vy. dk.
○	437	tan, lt.
●	413	pewter gray, dk.
✳	3778	terra cotta, lt.

Fabrics: ***Polo Shirt***—20-count linen used as waste canvas; ***Bookmark***—18-count cream Aida Ribband® with green trim from Leisure Arts

Stitch count:

Ruler	30H x 6W
Crayon	30H x 5W
Apple	15H x 12W
Pencil	35H x 4W

Design size:

Polo Shirt		
Ruler	20-count	3" x ⅝"
Crayon	20-count	3" x ½"
Pencil	20-count	3½" x ½"
Bookmark		
Ruler	18-count	1⅝" x ⅜"
Crayon	18-count	1⅝" x ⅜"
Apple	18-count	⅞" x ⅝"
Pencil	18-count	2" x ¼"

Polo Shirt (Photo is on page 13.)
Instructions: Cross stitch over two threads using three strands of floss. Backstitch using two strands 413. Stitch designs vertically, leaving ten threads between each.

Bookmark (Photo is on page 109.)
Instructions: Cross stitch using two strands of floss. Backstitch using one strand of floss. Make French knot for pencil lead using two strands 413. Center designs on fabric, leaving two squares between each.
Backstitch instructions:
437 apple stem
413 remainder of backstitching

WATERMELONS

	DMC	COLOR
■	310	black
X	319	pistachio, vy. dk.
I	894	carnation, vy. lt.
○	892	carnation, med.
·	772	pine green, lt.
S	318	steel gray, lt.

Fabrics: ***Sweatshirt***—14-count white Aida insert on white sweatshirt from The JanLynn® Corporation; ***Bookmark***—18-count cream Aida Ribband® with green trim from Leisure Arts

Stitch count:

Whole	15H x 22W
Quarter	13H x 16W
Half	9H x 22W
Half-eaten	9H x 22W
Gone	12H x 22W

Design size:

Sweatshirt		
Whole	14-count	1⅛" x 1⅝"
Quarter	14-count	1" x 1⅛"
Half	14-count	⅝" x 1⅝"
Half-eaten	14-count	⅝" x 1⅝"
Gone	14-count	⅞" x 1⅝"
Bookmark		
Whole	18-count	⅞" x 1¼"
Quarter	18-count	¾" x ⅞"
Half	18-count	½" x 1¼"
Half-eaten	18-count	½" x 1¼"
Gone	18-count	⅝" x 1¼"

Sweatshirt (Photo is on page 12.)
Instructions: Cross stitch using two strands of floss. Backstitch fork tines using one strand 318. Center middle motif and stitch motifs side by side, leaving ten squares between each.

Bookmark (Photo is on page 109.)
Instructions: Cross stitch using two strands of floss. Backstitch fork tines using one strand 318. Center motifs, leaving nine squares between each.

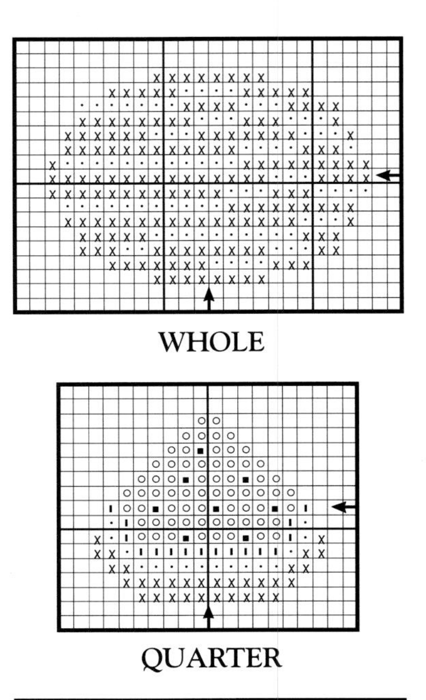

WHOLE

QUARTER

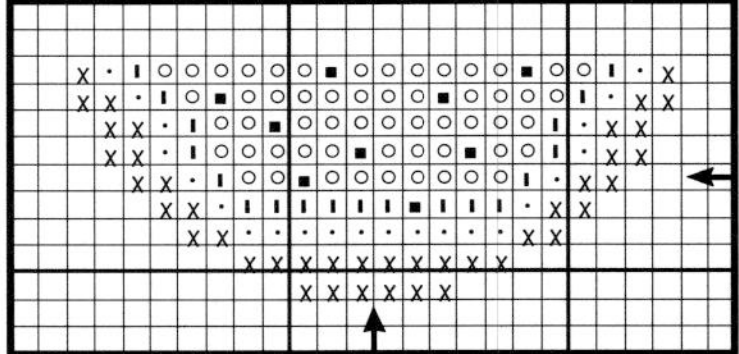

HALF

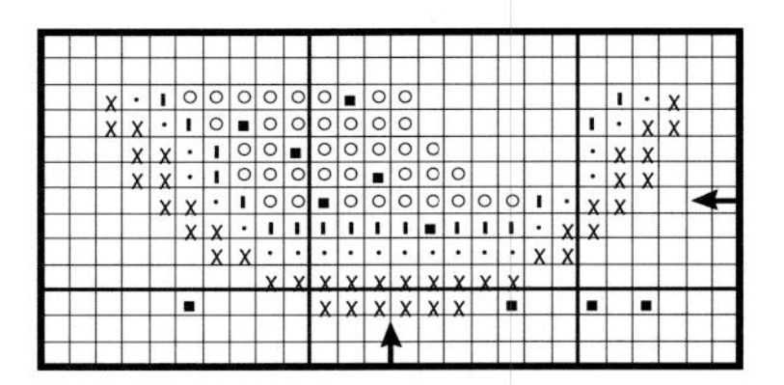

HALF-EATEN

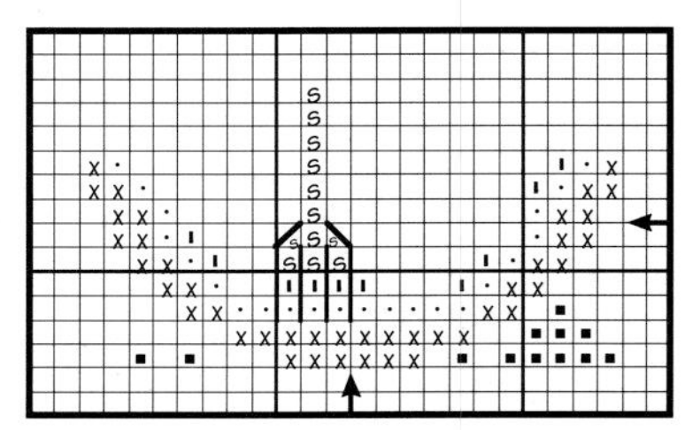

GONE

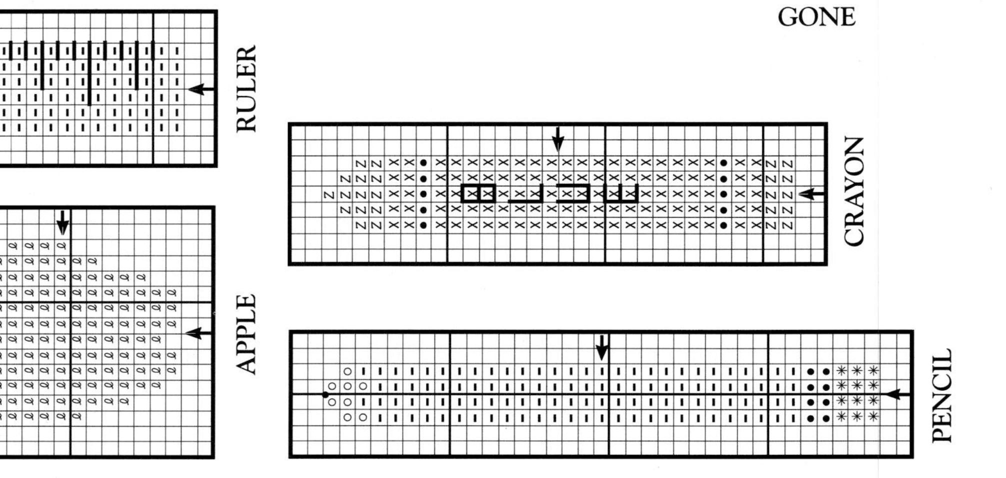

RULER

CRAYON

APPLE

PENCIL

Forget-me-not Bouquet

Today's young lady has at least one pair of men's boxer shorts to wear over her exercise and dance outfits! Add a feminine touch to this traditional, man's undergarment when you stitch a delicate floral bouquet in pale floss shades of blue, yellow, and green on one leg of her favorite pair. The garment will be a welcome addition to her wardrobe.

	DMC	COLOR
B	813	blue, lt.
=	744	yellow, pl.
L	913	Nile green, med.
bs	500	blue-green, vy. dk.

Fabrics: *Boxer Shorts and Coral Dress*—20-count linen used as waste canvas
Stitch count: 20H x 21W
Design size:
20-count 2" x 2"

Boxer Shorts (Shown below.)
Instructions: Cross stitch over two threads using three strands of floss. Backstitch using one strand of floss unless otherwise indicated. Stitch motif on boxer shorts 2" in from side seam and 2" up from hem.

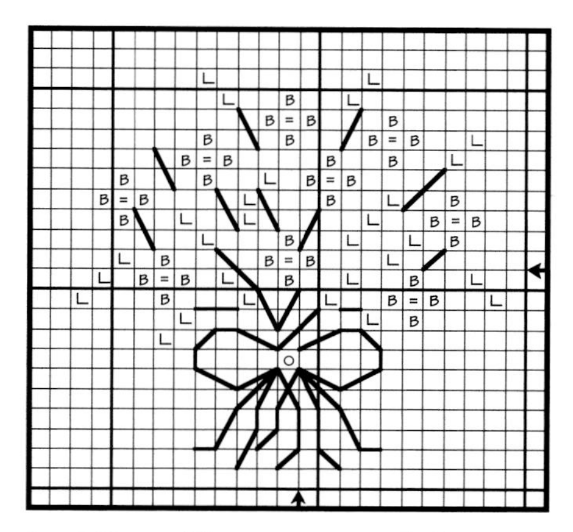

Coral Dress (Photo is on page 59.)
Instructions: Cross stitch over two threads using three strands of floss. Backstitch using one strand of floss unless otherwise indicated. Stitch design 1" down from neckline and 1" in from right sleeve seam. Stitch design 1" up from hem and 2½" in from left side seam.
Backstitch (bs) instructions:
813 bow (two strands)
500 remainder of backstitching

Vine Alphabet

Entwining vines and tiny flowers form decorative letters that are suitable for monogramming a variety of clothing and accessory items. Shown worked on a purchased scarf, the initials were stitched using 20-count linen in place of waste canvas.

	DMC	COLOR
X	503	blue-green, med.
•	501	blue-green, dk.
bs	500	blue-green, vy. dk.

Fabrics: ***Scarf*** —20-count linen used as waste canvas; ***Towel***—14-count ecru Park Avenue Fingertips™ towel from Charles Craft, Inc.; ***Tote Bag***—14-count Fiddler's Lite Not So Little Tote Bag from The JanLynn® Corporation

Stitch count:

A, J	22H x 17W
B, C, D, E, H, K, L, M, N, O, P, R, S, T, U, V, W, X, Y, Z	22H X 16W
F, G, Q	22H X 15W
I	22H x 11W
Border	7H x 23W

Design size:

20-count

A, J	2¼" x 1¾"
B, C, D, E, H, K, L, M, N, O, P, R, S, T, U, V, W, X, Y, Z	2¼" x 1⅝"
F, G, Q	2¼" x 1½"
I	2¼" x 1⅛"
Border	¾" x 2⅜"

14-count

A, J	1⅝" x 1¼"
B, C, D, E, H, K, L, M, N, O, P, R, S, T, U, V, W, X, Y, Z	1⅝" x 1⅛"
F, G, Q	1⅝" x 1"
I	1⅝" x ¾"
Border	½" x 1⅝"

Scarf

Instructions: Cross stitch over two threads using three strands of floss. Backstitch (bs) using two strands 500. Stitch letters 2" up from lower edge of scarf, leaving 12 threads between each.

Towel and Tote Bag (Photo is on page 112.)

Instructions: Cross stitch using three strands of floss. Backstitch (bs) using two strands 500. Center letters on cross-stitch fabric panel of towel, leaving three squares between each. Center letters 2" down from upper edge of tote, leaving ten squares between each.

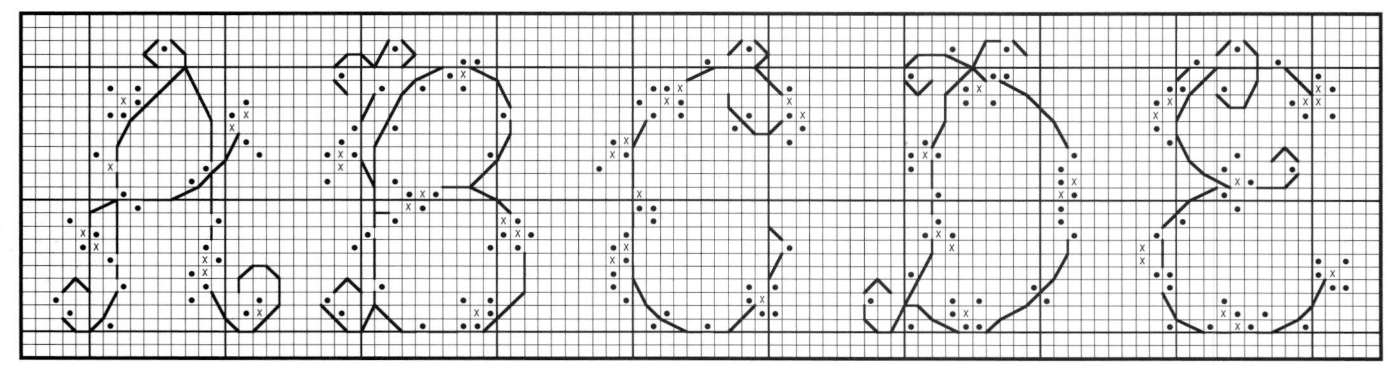

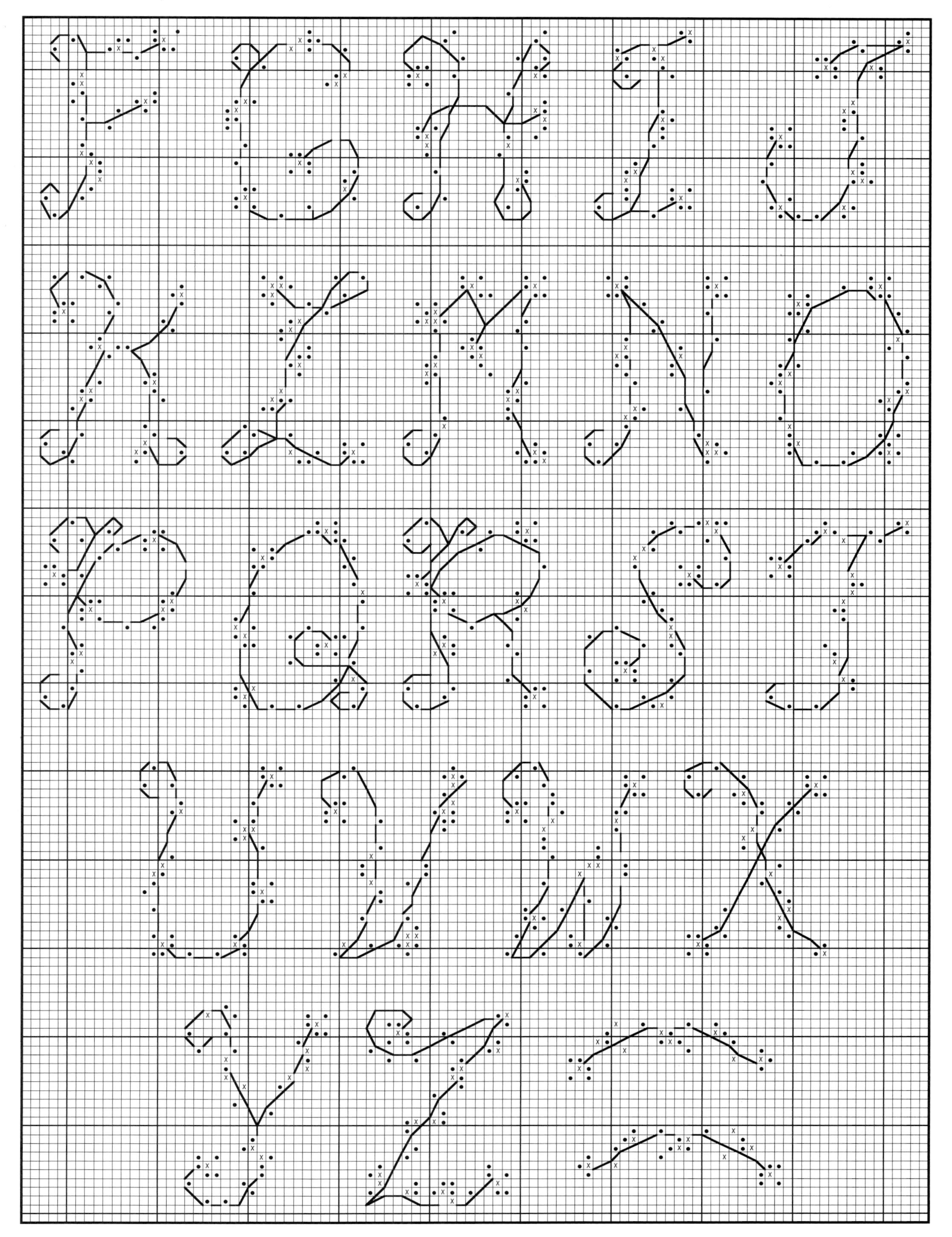

Sunflowers

Capture the warmth of the sun in bright yellow stitches that form a colorful sunflower. Work this vivid bloom on a white turtleneck and savor a touch of summer throughout the winter months.

	DMC	COLOR
Z	898	coffee brown, vy. dk.
O	743	yellow, med.
X	520	fern green, dk.
bs	782	topaz, med.

Fabric: 20-count linen used as waste canvas on white turtleneck
Stitch count: 25H x 17W
Design size:
20-count 2½" x 1¾"

Instructions: Cross stitch over two threads using three strands of floss. Backstitch using two strands of floss unless otherwise indicated. Stitch right motif 1½" down from shoulder seam and 2" in from sleeve seam. Stitch left motif 3" in from side seam and 2" up from hem in lower left corner of shirt.
Backstitch (bs) instructions:
782 flower petals
520 stems

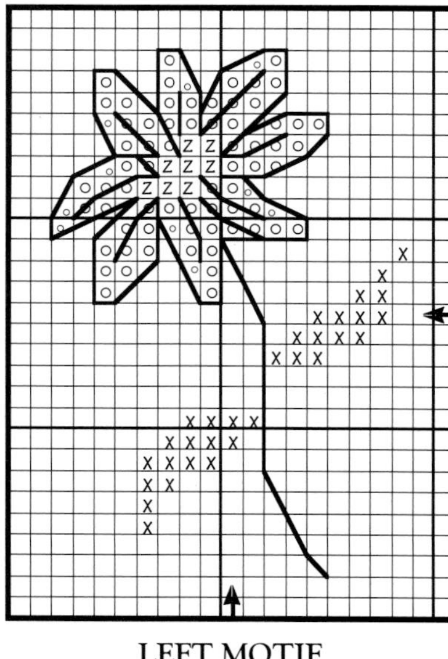

LEFT MOTIF

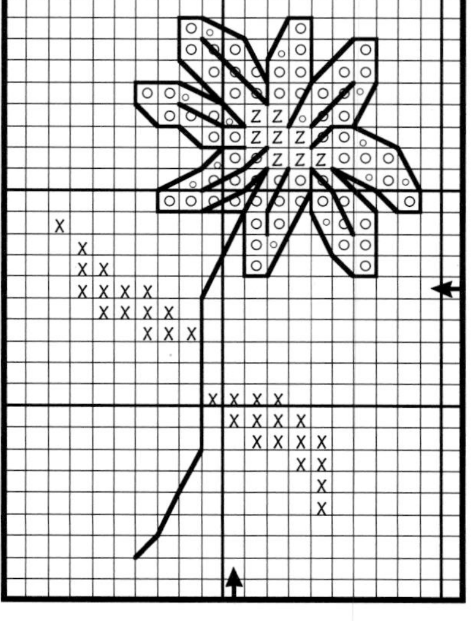

RIGHT MOTIF

Red Chilies

The vibrant colors of these red chili peppers add the perfect touch to a blue chambray front-button shirt. These "hot" accents are also featured with other Southwestern-inspired motifs on place mats and napkins, pictured on page 78.

	DMC	COLOR
•	321	red
○	946	burnt orange, med.
M	606	orange-red
bs	905	parrot green, dk.

Fabric: 20-count linen used as waste canvas on blue chambray shirt
Stitch count: 26H x 12W
Design size:
20-count 2⅝" x 1¼"

Instructions: Cross stitch over two threads using two strands of floss. Backstitch (bs) stems using two strands 905. Stitch design between buttonholes on front placket of shirt and horizontally on each sleeve cuff.

Pineapple Monogram

If you spend countless hours preparing meals and baking scrumptious goodies for your family and you revel in every single minute, this cook's apron is certain to be a favorite with you. In just a few hours of stitching, you can transform a basic garment protector into a monogrammed "treat" that you'll enjoy putting on each time you enter the kitchen.

	DMC	COLOR
•	731	olive, dk.
X	733	olive, med.
6	781	topaz, dk.
O	783	gold

Fabrics: ***Apron, Makeup Bag, and Umbrella***—20-count linen used as waste canvas
Stitch count:

Pineapple	18H x 14W	
Letter	14H x 14W	

Design size:

Pineapple	20-count	1⅞" x 1½"
Letter	20-count	1½" x 1½"

Apron
Instructions: Cross stitch over two threads using three strands of floss. Backstitch pineapples using two strands 731. Center letters 3" down from upper edge of apron, leaving six threads between each. Center pineapple above and below middle letter, leaving ten threads between letter and pineapple.

Makeup Bag (Photo is on page 116.)
Instructions: Cross stitch over two threads using four strands of floss. Do not stitch borders around letters. Center initials on side of bag, leaving four threads between each.

Umbrella (Photo is on page 116.)
Instructions: Cross stitch over two threads using four strands of floss. Center initials with borders on one panel of umbrella 3" up from lower edge, leaving four threads between each.

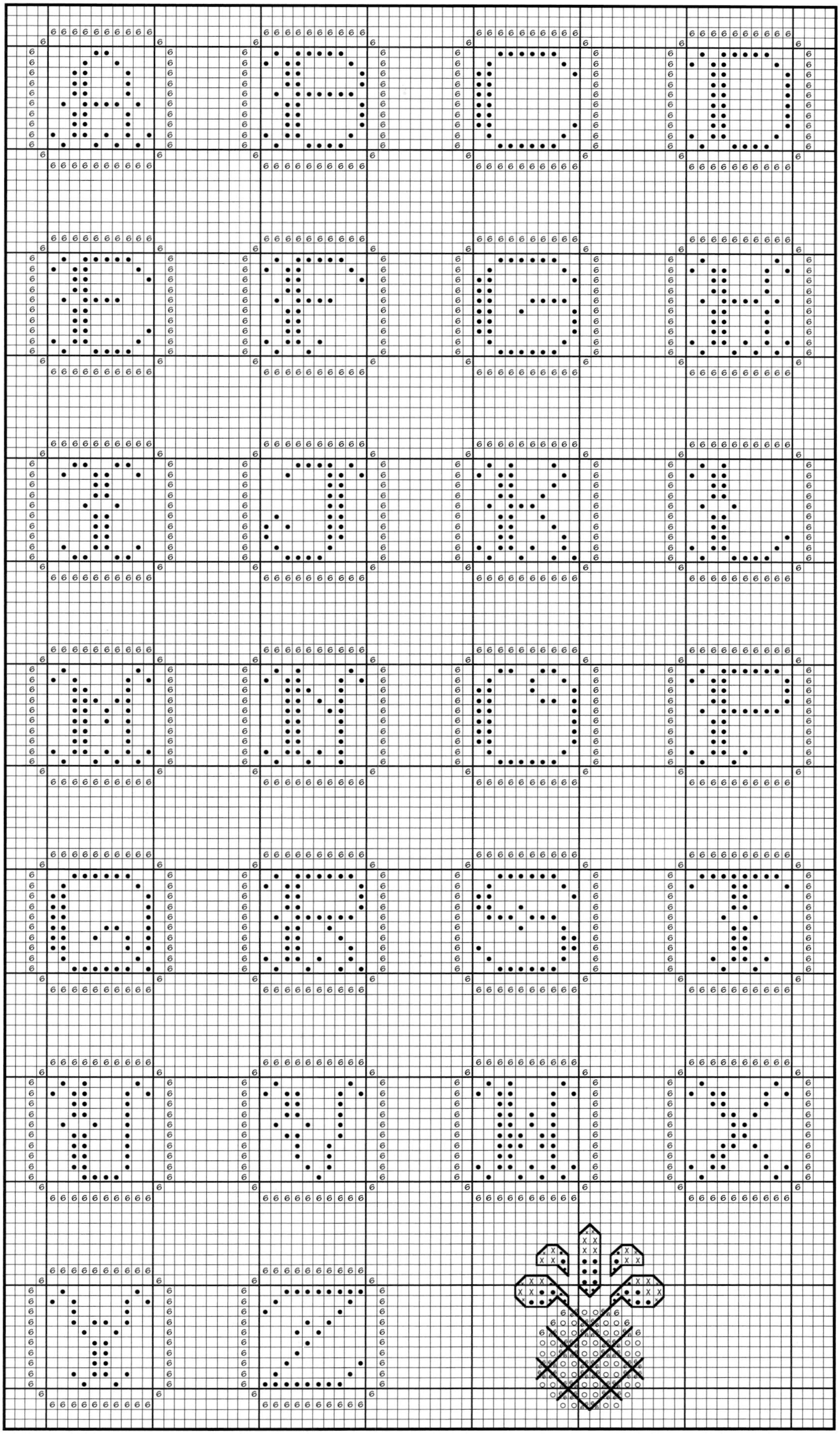

Acorn and Leaf

Greet fall with stitchery that makes a plain blouse a seasonal delight. Worked between the buttons of a purchased shirt, the acorn and leaf motifs will convey your love for this colorful time of the year. Complete your creation with a single acorn stitched at one tip of the collar and you'll have autumn-inspired fashion apparel throughout the leaf-falling season.

	DMC	COLOR
X	3781	mocha brown, dk.
O	781	topaz, dk.
\\	721	spice, med.
ℓ	743	yellow, med.

Fabric: 27-count linen used as waste canvas on white cotton blouse

Stitch count:

Acorn	9H x 8W
Leaf	13H x 6W

Design size:

Acorn	27-count	⅝" x ⅝"
Leaf	27-count	1" x ½"

Instructions: Cross stitch over two threads using two strands of floss. Backstitch leaf stem using one strand 3781. Beginning with *Leaf* design, alternate *Acorn* and *Leaf* designs between buttonholes on front placket of blouse. Stitch *Acorn* at left tip of collar.

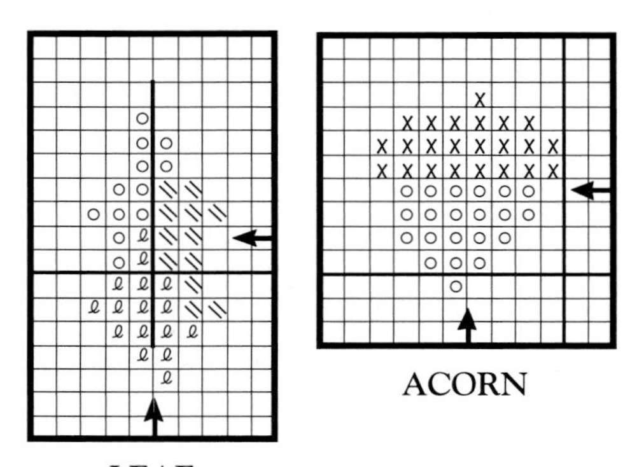

LEAF

ACORN

Holly Leaves

Giving a blouse festive appeal is easy! Select a white blouse at a store or choose one from your closet. Using linen, stitch the *Holly Leaves* design between the buttonholes. Sew on red buttons to represent holly berries for a top that boasts a designer look at a fraction of the cost.

	DMC	COLOR
•	936	avocado, vy. dk.
6	469	avocado
/	471	avocado, vy. lt.

Fabric: 32-count linen used as waste canvas on white cotton blouse
Stitch count: 24H x 16W
Design size:
32-count 1½" x 1"

Instructions: Cross stitch over two threads using two strands of floss. Stitch *Holly Leaves* just above buttonholes on front placket of blouse. Replace buttons with red buttons to resemble holly berries.

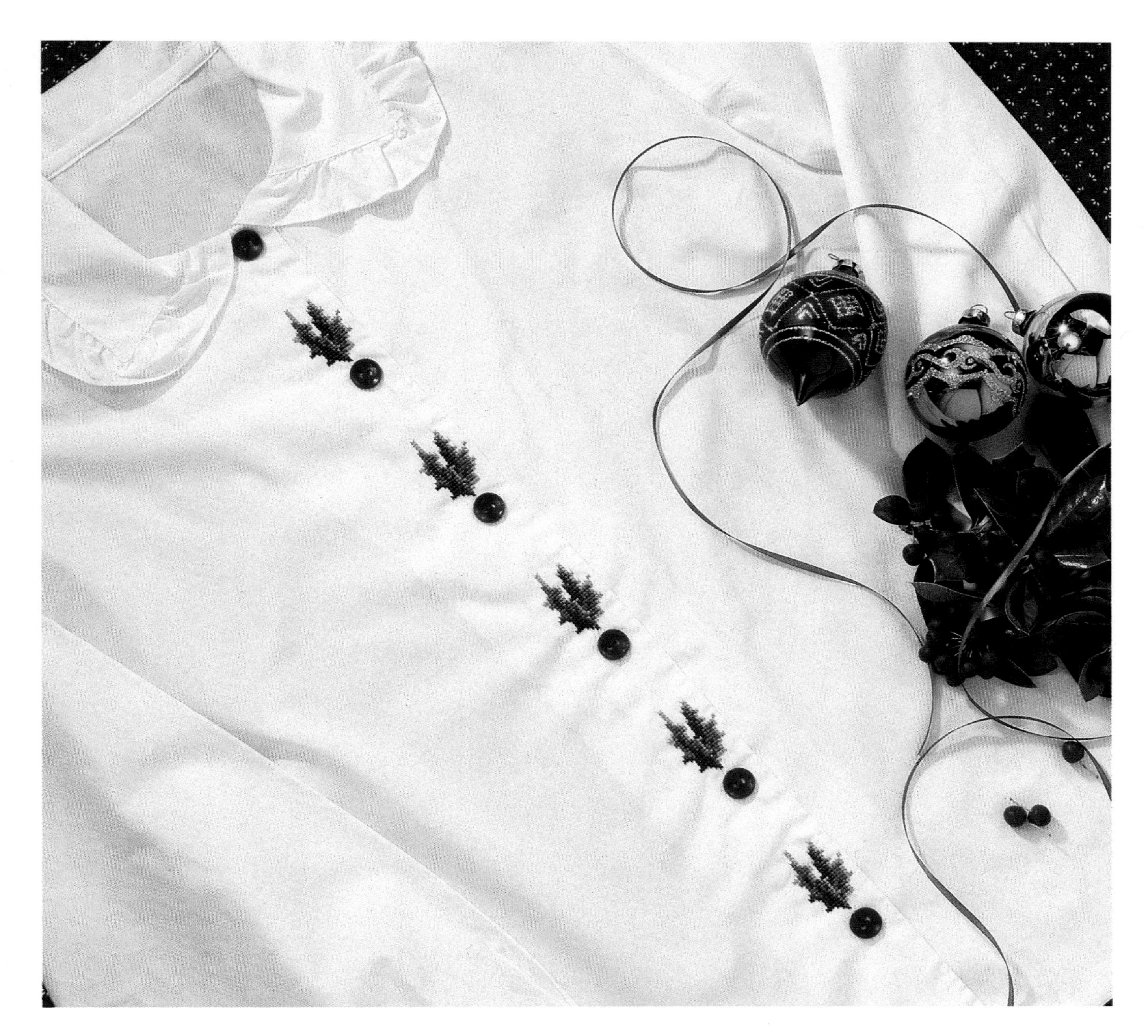

For Kids

Ready-made items for children and babies—from overalls to tote bags, from sleepers to cuddly blankets—take on unforgettable charm when embellished with cute, just-for-kids cross stitch. Use your skills with the needle to decorate a gift to welcome a little one into the world or to enhance an outfit for a special niece or nephew.

Fun with Color!

Kids take pride in things Mommy makes for them, especially when those things make them the center of attention at school. What better way to show off than with friendly dinosaurs, a bright sailboat, or a happy-face sun? These designs will also be cute on lunch sacks and book bags, as well as on T-shirts for summer. Use the dinosaur trio to turn a cross-stitch bib into an eye-catching clothing protector for a family preschooler or to make a wonderful shower gift for a friend who's expecting.

DINOSAURS

	DMC	COLOR
6	552	violet, dk.
X	666	red, bt.
▲	797	royal blue
○	970	pumpkin, lt.
ℓ	700	green, bt.
●	307	lemon

Fabrics: ***Baby Bib***—14-count white Aida insert on Deluxe Baby Bib from Charles Craft, Inc.; ***Shirt***—6-count royal blue thermal shirt

Stitch count:

Dinosaurs	26H x 93W
Yellow Dinosaur	15H x 32W

Design size:

Dinosaurs	14-count	1⅞" x 6⅝"
Yellow Dinosaur	6-count	2½" x 5⅜"

Baby bib

Instructions: Cross stitch using two strands of floss. Center *Dinosaurs* on cross-stitch fabric band of bib.

Shirt

Instructions: Cross stitch using four strands of floss. Stitch over squares of thermal fabric. Center yellow dinosaur 2" down from neckline.

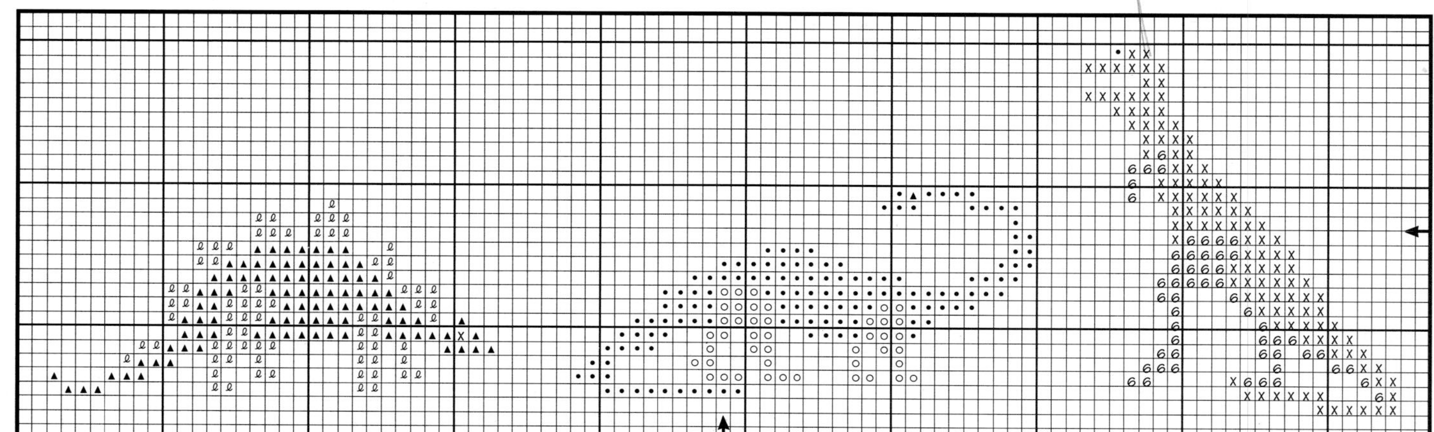

SAILBOAT AND ANCHOR

	DMC	COLOR
F	666	red, bt.
P	333	blue-violet, dk.
B	798	delft, dk.
G	700	green, bt.
Y	307	lemon
O	608	orange
S	300	mahogany, vy. dk.
•	993	aqua, lt.
bs	310	black

Fabric: 27-count linen used as waste canvas on white turtleneck

Stitch count:

Anchor	12H x 8W
Sailboat	18H x 22W

Design size:

Anchor	27-count	1¾" x 1¼"
Sailboat	27-count	2⅝" x 3¼"

Instructions: Cross stitch over four threads using six strands of floss. Backstitch using two strands of floss. Backstitch *Anchor* using three strands 310. Center *Sailboat* 2" down from neckline. Stitch *Anchor* on collar 1½" to the right of center.

Backstitch (bs) instructions:

310	anchor
300	mast
993	waves
700	boom under large sail
608	boom under small sail
333	top of large sail where it connects to mast
307	top of small sail where it connects to mast

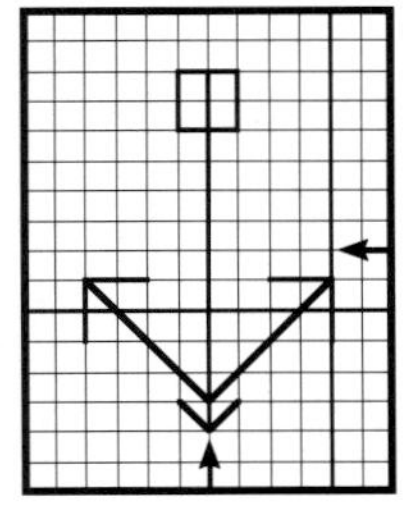

ANCHOR

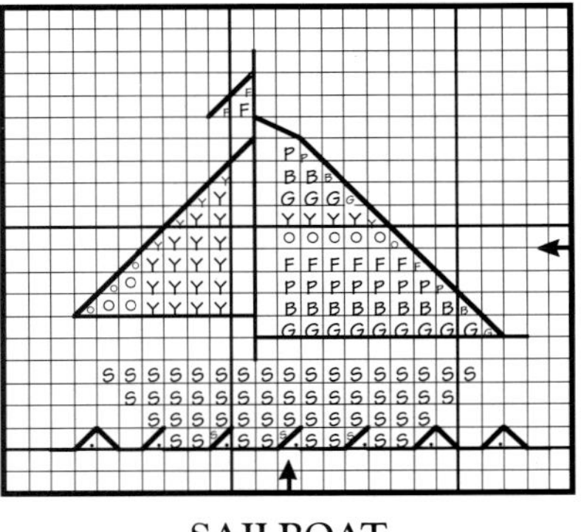

SAILBOAT

SUNSHINE FUN

	DMC	COLOR
3	825	blue, dk.
O	701	green, lt.
/	444	lemon, dk.
X	740	tangerine
•	321	red
■	310	black

Fabric: 20-count linen used as waste canvas on fanny pack

Stitch count: 20H x 20W

Design size:

20-count 2" x 2"

Instructions: Cross stitch over two threads using four strands of floss. Backstitch using two strands of floss. Center design on top flap.

Backstitch instructions:

444	sun's rays
310	remainder of backstitching

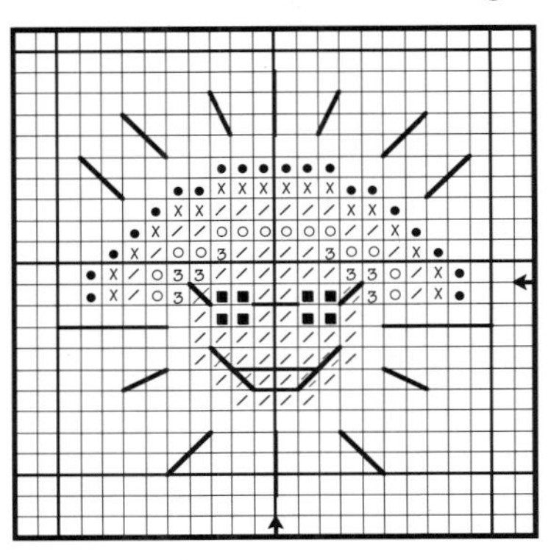

Noah's Ark

Every child likes hearing the story of Noah and his ark and giggles thinking about all those animals gathered in one place! Stitch *Noah's Ark* as shown on a red sweatshirt or work the motifs individually on winter warmers. The ark rests at the end of a cozy muffler, and the animals march across the front of a knitted cap. Use your imagination when deciding where to place these charming critters and expect your handiwork to make these items your children's favorites.

	DMC	COLOR
V	3750	antique blue, vy. dk.
Z	422	hazelnut, lt.
▲	310	black
•	white	white
G	703	chartreuse

Fabrics: ***Sweatshirt***—27-count linen used as waste canvas; ***Scarf and Cap***—20-count linen used as waste canvas

Stitch count:

Noah's Ark	22H x 115W
Ark	22H x 27W
Animals	11H x 95W

Design size:

Noah's Ark	27-count	1⅝" x 8⅝"
Ark	20-count	2¼" x 2¾"
Animals	20-count	1⅛" x 9⅝"

Instructions: Cross stitch over two threads using two strands of floss. Backstitch using two strands of floss. Make French knots for noses and eyes where • appears at intersecting grid lines using two strands 310, wrapping floss around needle once. Center design 1½" down from neckline of shirt. Center ark motif on one end of scarf 2" up from fringed edge. Center animals on band of cap, leaving five spaces between each.

Backstitch (bs) instructions:

422	birds' beaks and legs
310	remainder of backstitching

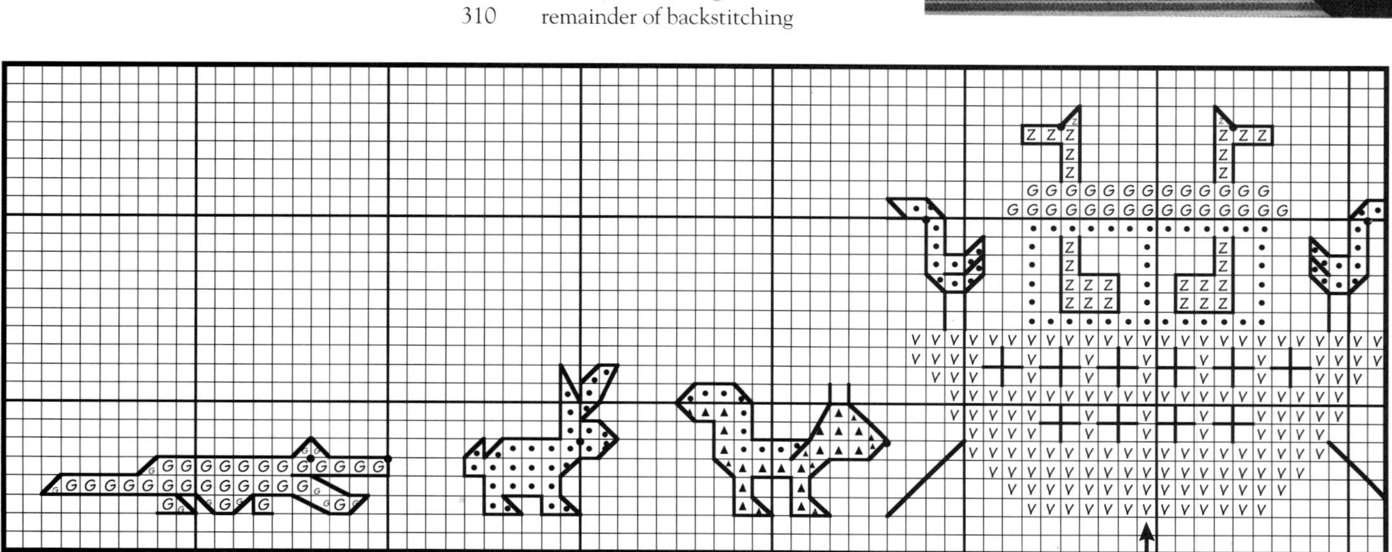

Shaded portion indicates overlap from previous page.

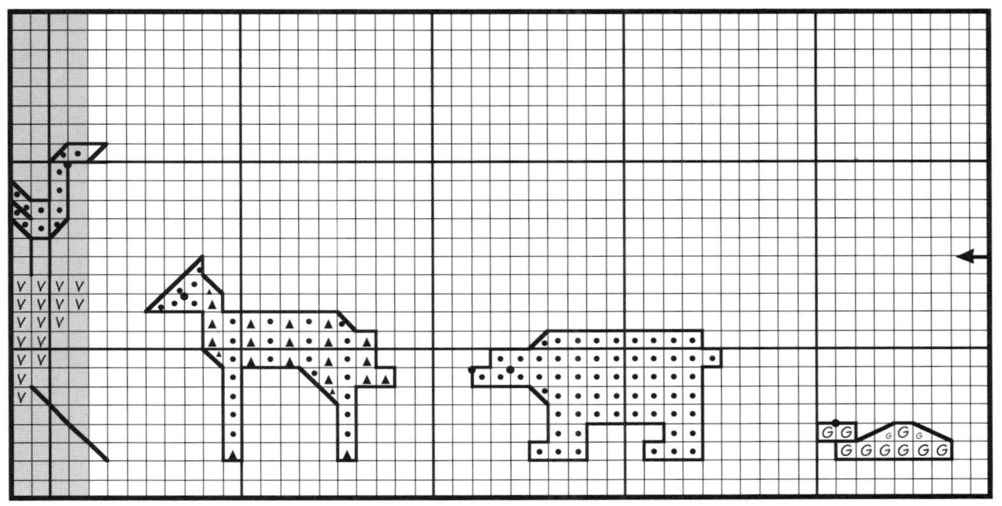

Practical
Handbook

Rainbow Alphabet

The rainbow, a wonder of nature, was the inspiration for the *Rainbow Alphabet*, which includes two color schemes: primary brights and gentle pastels. The letters are suitable for personalizing an assortment of children's clothing and accessories, as well as the smallest baby garments. Primary-colored letters, worked on an umbrella and a fanny pack, far left, look especially good with bold colors while the pastels blend beautifully with pieces constructed of pale or white fabrics. Choose either the primaries or the pastels and whip up a fantastic birthday present for a niece or nephew or a gift for a newborn. Chart begins on page 32.

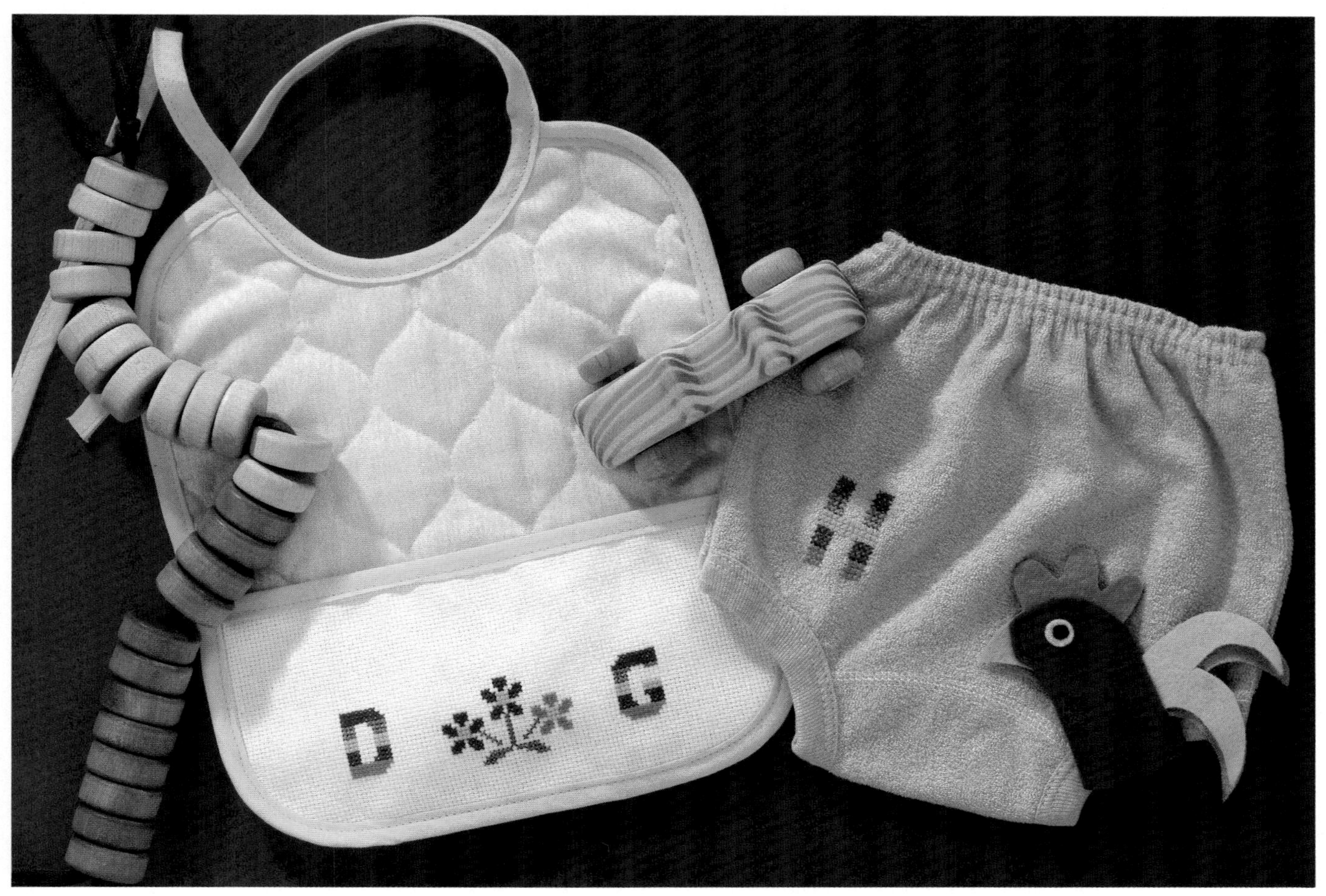

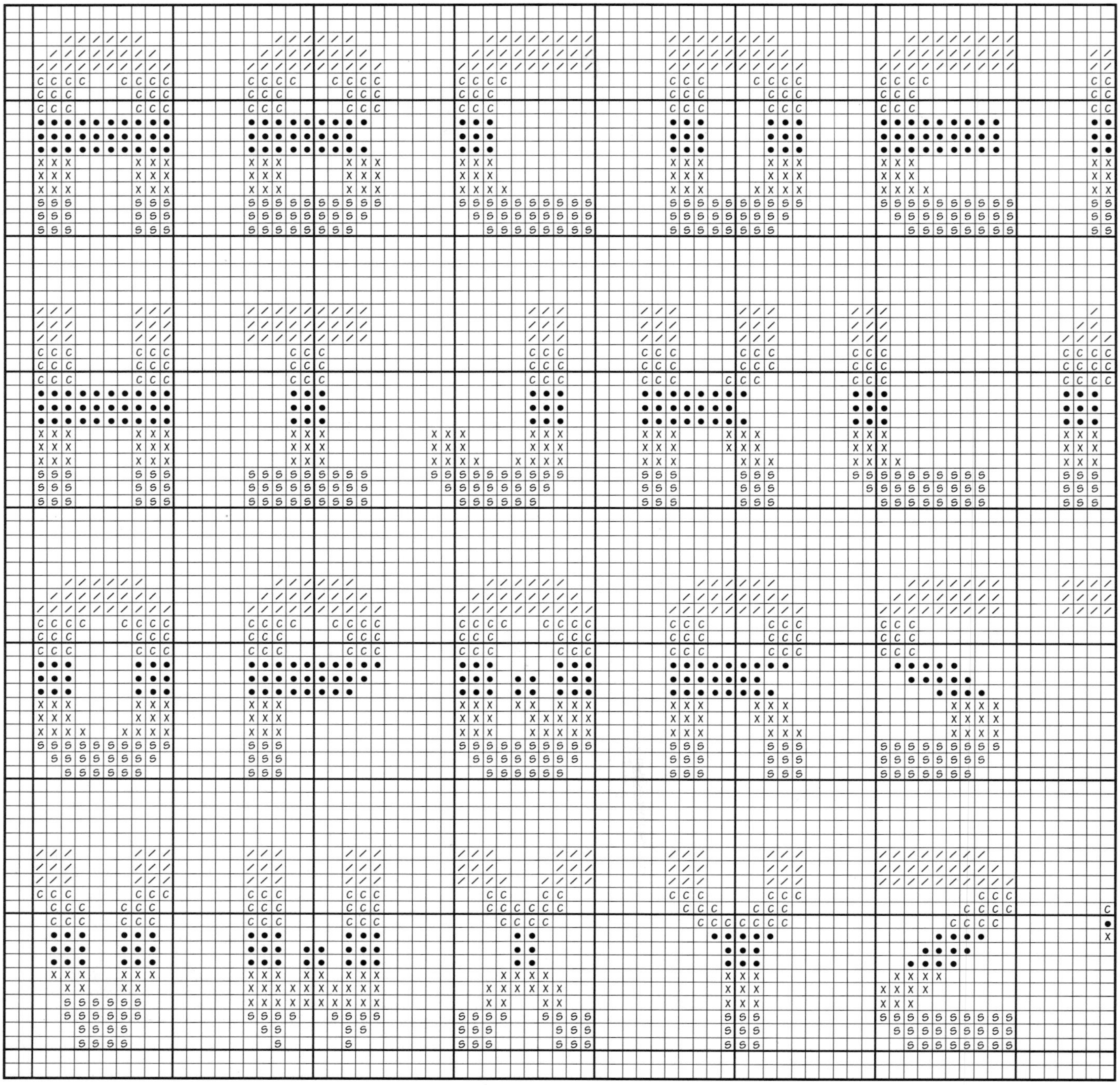

Shaded portion indicates overlap from previous page.

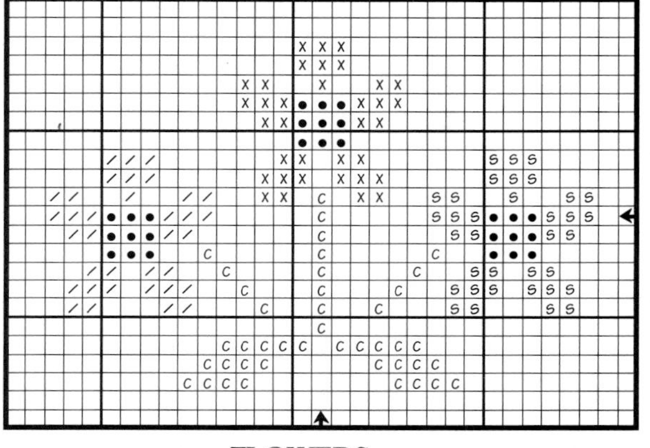

FLOWERS

RAINBOW ALPHABET

Primary Colors

	DMC	COLOR
/	321	red
C	702	kelly green
•	972	canary, dp.
X	312	navy, lt.
S	970	pumpkin, lt.

NOTE: When stitching on red fabric, substitute white floss for 321 red.

Pastel Colors

	DMC	COLOR
/	776	pink, med.
C	966	baby green, med.
•	445	lemon, lt.
X	827	blue, vy. lt.
S	210	lavender, med.

Fabrics: ***Bib***—14-count white Aida insert on yellow-trimmed bib from The JanLynn® Corporation; ***Romper and Socks***—28-count linen used as waste canvas; ***Umbrella, Fanny Pack, and Diaper Pants***—20-count linen used as waste canvas

Stitch count:

Letters	15H x 10W
Circle	5H x 5W
Flowers	19H x 29W

Design size:

Letters	14-count	1¼" x ¾"
	20-count	1½" x 1"
	28-count	1¼" x ¾"
Circle	20-count	½" x ½"
Flowers	14-count	1⅜" x 2¼"

Bib

Instructions: Cross stitch using two strands of floss. Center *Flowers* on cross-stitch fabric band of bib. Stitch letters on either side of *Flowers*, leaving 12 squares between letters and *Flowers*.

Romper and Socks

Instructions: Cross stitch over two threads using three strands of floss. On romper, stitch letters on either side of chest 2" down from shoulder seams. Center letters on outer side of sock cuff.

Umbrella, Fanny Pack, and Diaper Pants

Instructions: Cross stitch over two threads using three strands of floss. Stitch letters and circle on one panel of umbrella, leaving twenty threads between each motif. Center name on front of pack, leaving fourteen threads between each letter. Stitch letter on back of diaper pants 1" in from side seam and 1¼" up from leg binding.

Le Clic

Water's Edge Favorites

Great for those sunny days at the beach or giggly girls' poolside parties, the *Sea Life* and *At the Beach* designs, stitched on purchased bags, make unique carryalls for fun-in-the-sun necessities. The *Bright Sunglasses* design adorns a zippered denim bag, below, that will be just right when a small tote is needed and also can be used as a casual summertime purse. Older girls will like these "cool" shades for embellishing a cover-up or oversized T-shirt. Charts for *At the Beach* and *Bright Sunglasses* are on page 36. Charts for *Sea Life* begin on page 10.

AT THE BEACH

	DMC	COLOR
•	white	white
o	608	orange
y	725	topaz
X	701	green, lt.
S	535	ash gray, vy. lt.
6	825	blue, dk.
■	310	black

Fabric: 20-count linen used as waste canvas on fuchsia tote
Stitch count: 67H x 37W
Design size:
20-count 6¾" x 3¾"

Instructions: Cross stitch over two threads using three strands of floss. Backstitch using two strands of floss. Make French knot on tip of radio antenna using two strands 535, wrapping floss around needle once. Center design on side of tote bag.

Backstitch instructions:

725	sunglasses frames
535	radio antenna
310	remainder of radio, strap on camera
white	drinking straw
701	lettering on lotion bottle

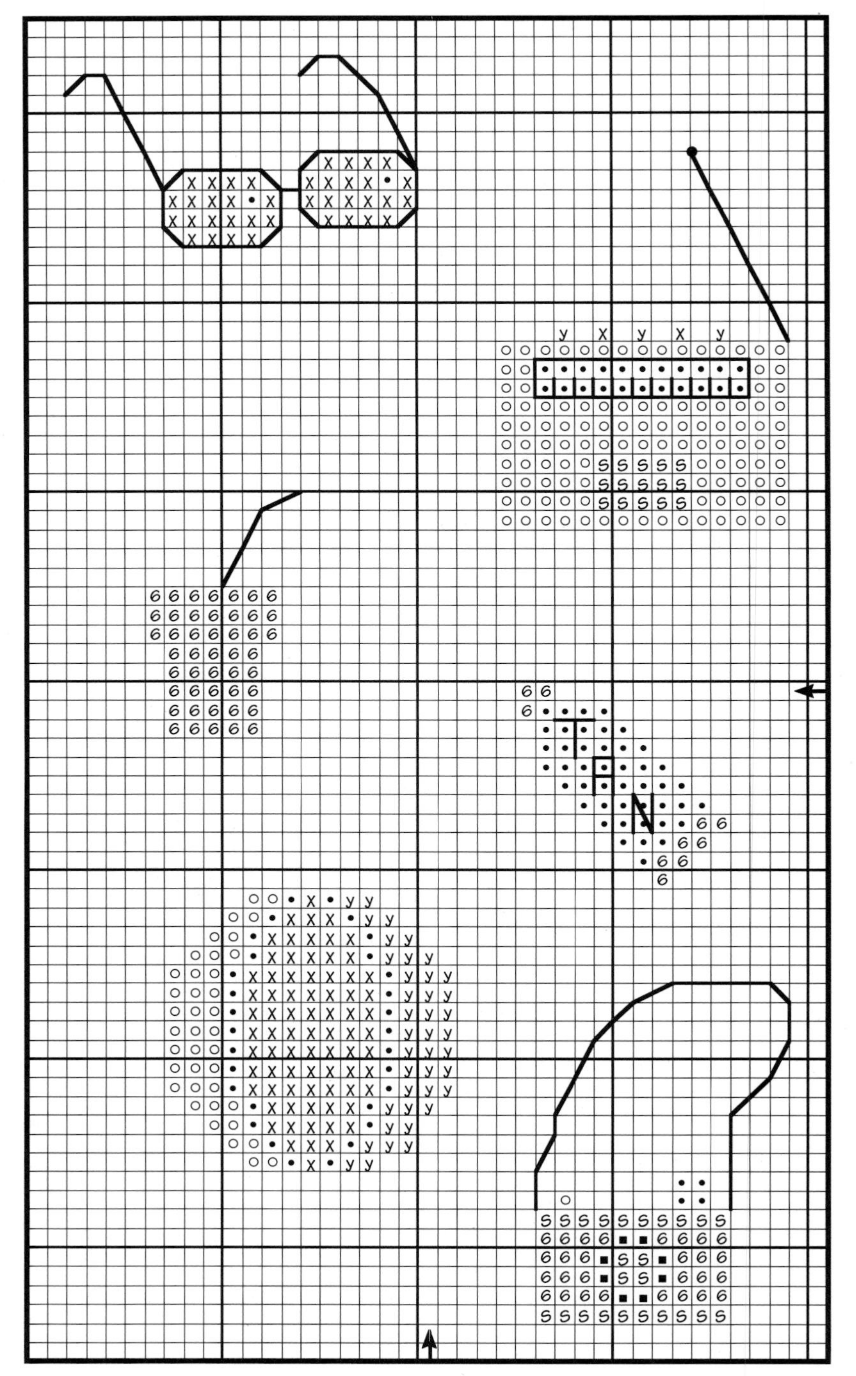

AT THE BEACH

BRIGHT SUNGLASSES

	DMC	COLOR
•	3777	terra cotta, vy. dk.
X	444	lemon, dk.
	OR	
X	704	chartreuse, bt.
	OR	
X	996	electric blue, med.

NOTE: The same chart is used to stitch three pairs of sunglasses, each in a different color.

Fabric: 20-count linen used as waste canvas on blue denim bag
Stitch count: 13H x 24W
Design size:
20-count 1⅜" x 2½"

Instructions: Cross stitch over two threads using four strands of floss. Center sunglasses on side of denim bag. Repeat design on either side in different colors, turning design to be slightly angled.

BRIGHT SUNGLASSES

Tooth Fairy

If all your little one wants right now is two front teeth, this tiny pillow will provide the perfect storage spot for those lost baby teeth. Tuck them safely inside the pocket while waiting for the tooth fairy to visit and watch the excitement that unfolds in the morning when your child finds the shiny coins left behind! Turn to page 142 for finishing instructions.

	DMC	COLOR
P	552	violet, dk.
B	809	delft
W	964	sea green, lt.
S	948	peach flesh, vy. lt.
bs	310	black

Fabric: 18-count white Aida
Stitch count: 21H x 30W
Design size:
18-count 1⅛" x 1⅝"

Instructions: Cross stitch using four strands of floss. Backstitch (bs) using two strands 310. Make French knots where ● appears at intersecting grid lines using two strands 310, wrapping floss around needle once.

Sleepy Time Stitchery

Shhhh! Baby is sleeping, and Mom is stitching. Send your cutie off to slumberland in this cuddly sleeper trimmed with the *Sweet Dreams* design or, when the weather is warmer, in a comfy shirt decorated with a pair of ducklings. The *Counting Sheep* pillow, hung on the front door, lets visitors know not to ring the bell. When used inside, it reminds older siblings that quiet time must be observed.

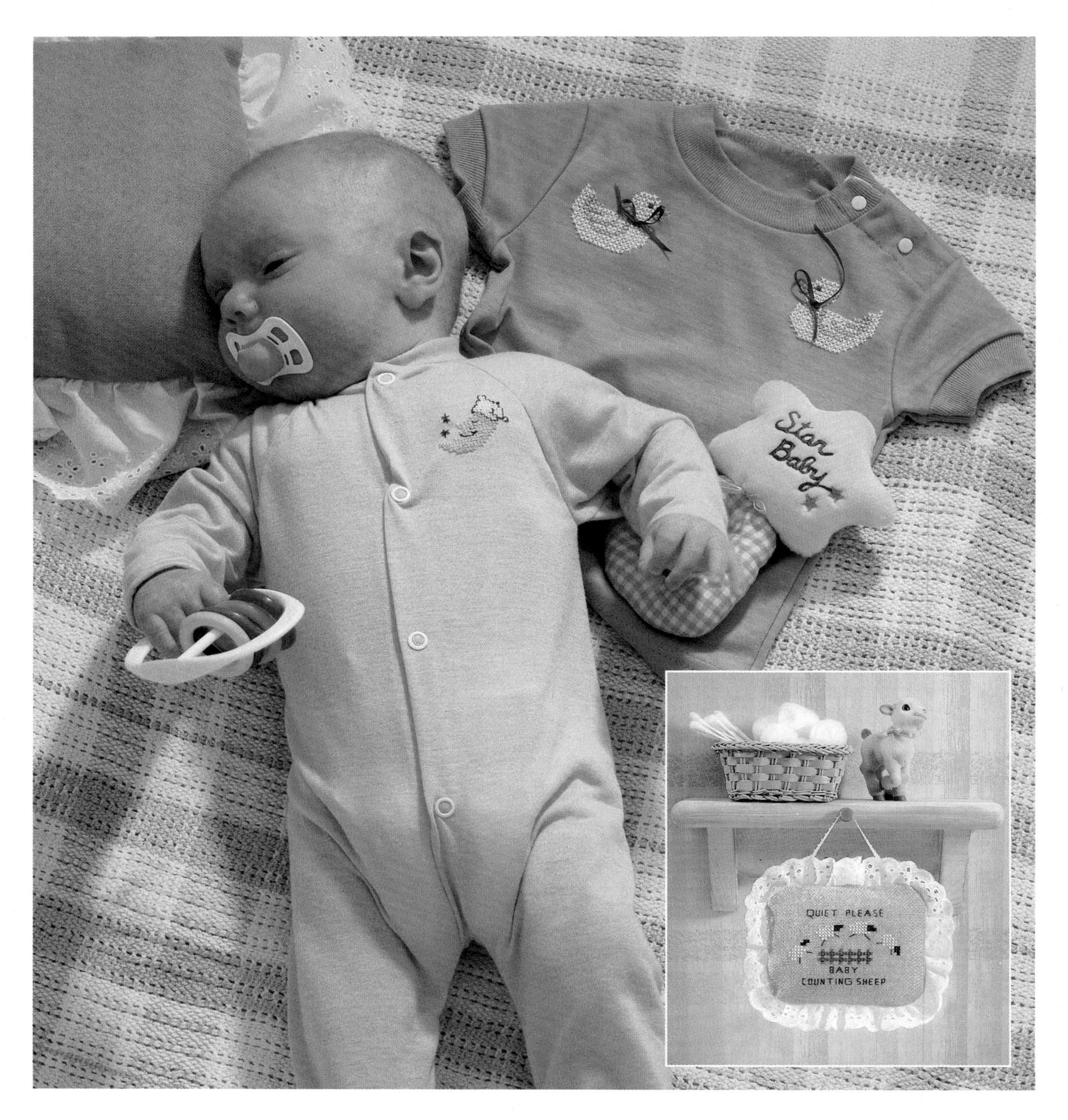

COUNTING SHEEP

COUNTING SHEEP

	DMC	COLOR
S	white	white
▲	780	topaz, vy. dk.
•	310	black

Fabric: 25-count Wedgewood Lugana® from Zweigart®
Stitch count: 25H x 37W
Design size:
25-count 2" x 3"

Instructions: Cross stitch over two threads using two strands of floss. Backstitch using one strand 310. Finishing instructions are on page 142.

DUCKLING FACING RIGHT

DUCKLING FACING LEFT

DUCKLINGS

	DMC	COLOR
/	white	white
3	415	pearl gray
○	740	tangerine
■	792	cornflower, dk.

Fabric: 20-count linen used as waste canvas on blue shirt
Stitch count: 16H x 20W
Design size:
20-count 1⅝" x 2"

Instructions: Cross stitch over two threads using three strands of floss. Stitch motifs 1" in from each sleeve seam and 1" down from neckline. When stitching is complete, tack 1/16"-wide blue satin ribbon bow where • appears on ducklings' necks.

SWEET DREAMS

	DMC	COLOR
X	444	lemon, dk.
I	307	lemon
/	white	white
+	762	pearl gray, vy. lt.
○	776	pink, med.
bs	791	cornflower, vy. dk.

Fabric: 27-count linen used as waste canvas on blue sleeper
Stitch count: 20H x 22W
Design size:
27-count 1½" x 1⅝"
Instructions: Cross stitch over two threads using two strands of floss. Backstitch (bs) hat, face, and stars using one strand 791. Center design on left side of sleeper 2" down from neckline.

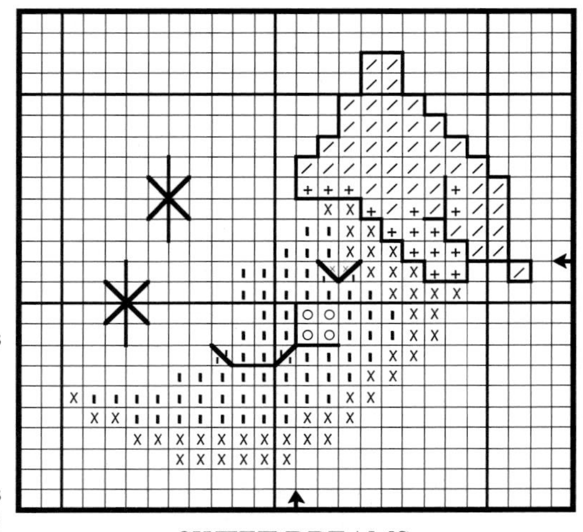

SWEET DREAMS

Boys' Toys

A boy's first serious vehicle is his roaring tricycle! This treasured three-wheeler becomes his race car, fiery steed, army tank, or spaceship. It takes him to all the imaginary places he dreams of. For him, a special riding shirt with a stitched rendition of his "adventure-mobile" is in order. For added appeal, create the design in colors to match his tricycle. The *School Bus* design will be perfect for trimming back-to-class pieces. The *Soccer Ball* design, worked above the chest pocket of a knit top, will tell everyone who sees him wearing it that this athlete loves to play soccer. Charts are on page 42.

SCHOOL BUS

SOCCER BALL

	DMC	COLOR
S	310	black
I	white	white

Fabric: 20-count linen used as waste canvas on red shirt
Stitch count: 16H x 16W
Design size:
20-count 1⅝" x 1⅝"

Instructions: Cross stitch over two threads using three strands of floss. Backstitch using one strand 310. Center design ¼" above pocket.

SCHOOL BUS

	DMC	COLOR
6	743	yellow, med.
+	321	red

Fabric: 20-count linen used as waste canvas on black sweatshirt
Stitch count: 24H x 43W
Design size:
20-count 2½" x 4⅜"

Instructions: Cross stitch over two threads using three strands of floss. Backstitch using two strands 743. Center design 1¼" down from neckline.

NEON TRICYCLE

	DMC	COLOR
3	606	orange-red
•	996	electric blue, med.
X	907	parrot green, lt.
+	307	lemon

Fabric: 20-count linen used as waste canvas on magenta shirt
Stitch count: 16H x 17W
Design size:
20-count 1⅝" x 1¾"

Instructions: Cross stitch over two threads using four strands of floss. Center design 1" above pocket.

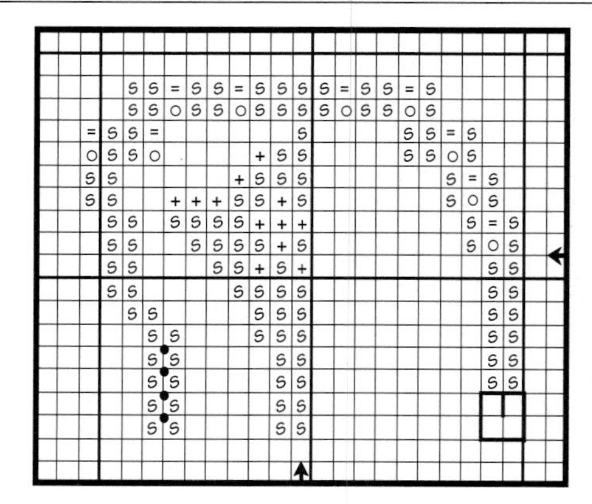

HOLSTER

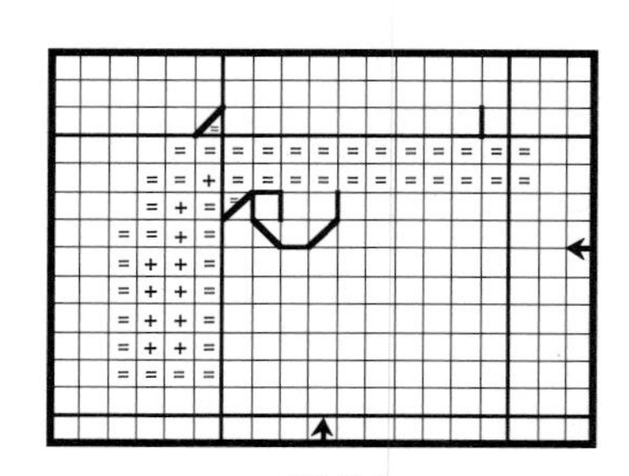

GUN

Five motifs form a collection for your Wild West hero. From a "ten-gallon" hat to a stitched sheriff's badge, these adorable add-ons will make him feel like a real cowboy from head to toe. Work them on a turtleneck, a book bag, an overnight tote, or anywhere you want to put the flavor of the West for your little buckaroo.

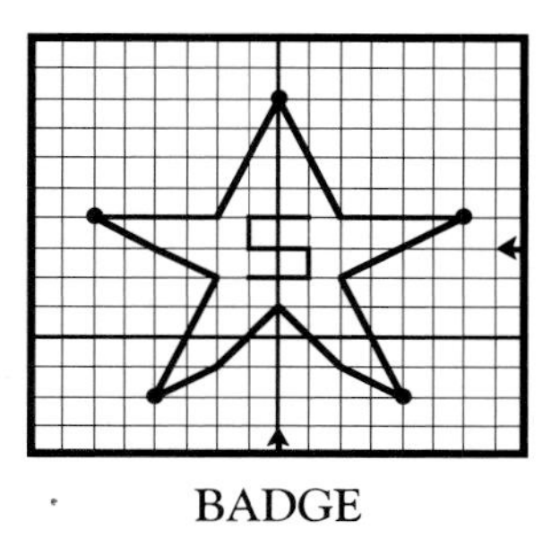

BADGE

BOOT

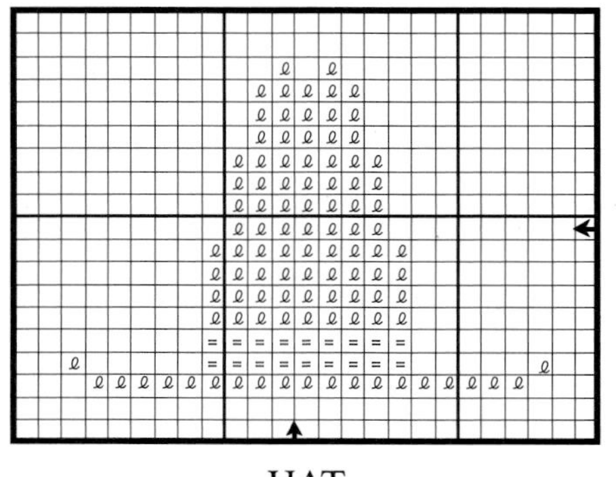

HAT

	DMC	COLOR
=	3799	pewter gray, dk.
S	869	hazelnut, vy. dk.
ℓ	436	tan
o	676	old gold, lt.
+	927	gray-green, med.

Fabric: 27-count linen used as waste canvas on turquoise turtleneck

Stitch count:

Holster	16H x 21W
Gun	10H x 15W
Badge	10H x 12W
Boot	17H x 16W
Hat	15H x 21W

Design size:

27-count

Holster	1⅛" x 1⅝"
Gun	¾" x 1⅛"
Badge	¾" x ⅞"
Boot	1¼" x 1¼"
Hat	1⅛" x 1⅝"

Instructions: Cross stitch over two threads using two strands of floss. Backstitch using two strands of floss. Make French knots where • appears at intersecting grid lines using two strands of floss, wrapping floss around needle once. Referring to photo, center middle motif 2" down from neckline. Stitch remaining motifs on either side of middle motif, leaving 7 threads between each.

Backstitch instructions:

3799	holster buckle, S on badge, all backstitching on gun
927	remainder of backstitching on badge

French knot instructions:

3799	holes on holster belt
927	tips of badge

Posy Border

There is nothing so sweet for embellishing baby things as a simple floral border. Using a repeating pattern that can be accomplished with a few passes of the needle, you can produce a pleasing ensemble in only a few hours. Work the border as shown or choose colors that complement the nursery or a special outfit. Chart is on page 46.

Floral Alphabet

Fantastic for decorating items for babies and girls, the *Floral Alphabet* is shown placed in the corner of a cozy pastel blanket with a border. The design will set off a young lady's Sunday dress when worked on the cuffs of lace-edged socks. Use floss colors to match her frilly finery, and she'll be set for a special occasion! Chart begins on page 46.

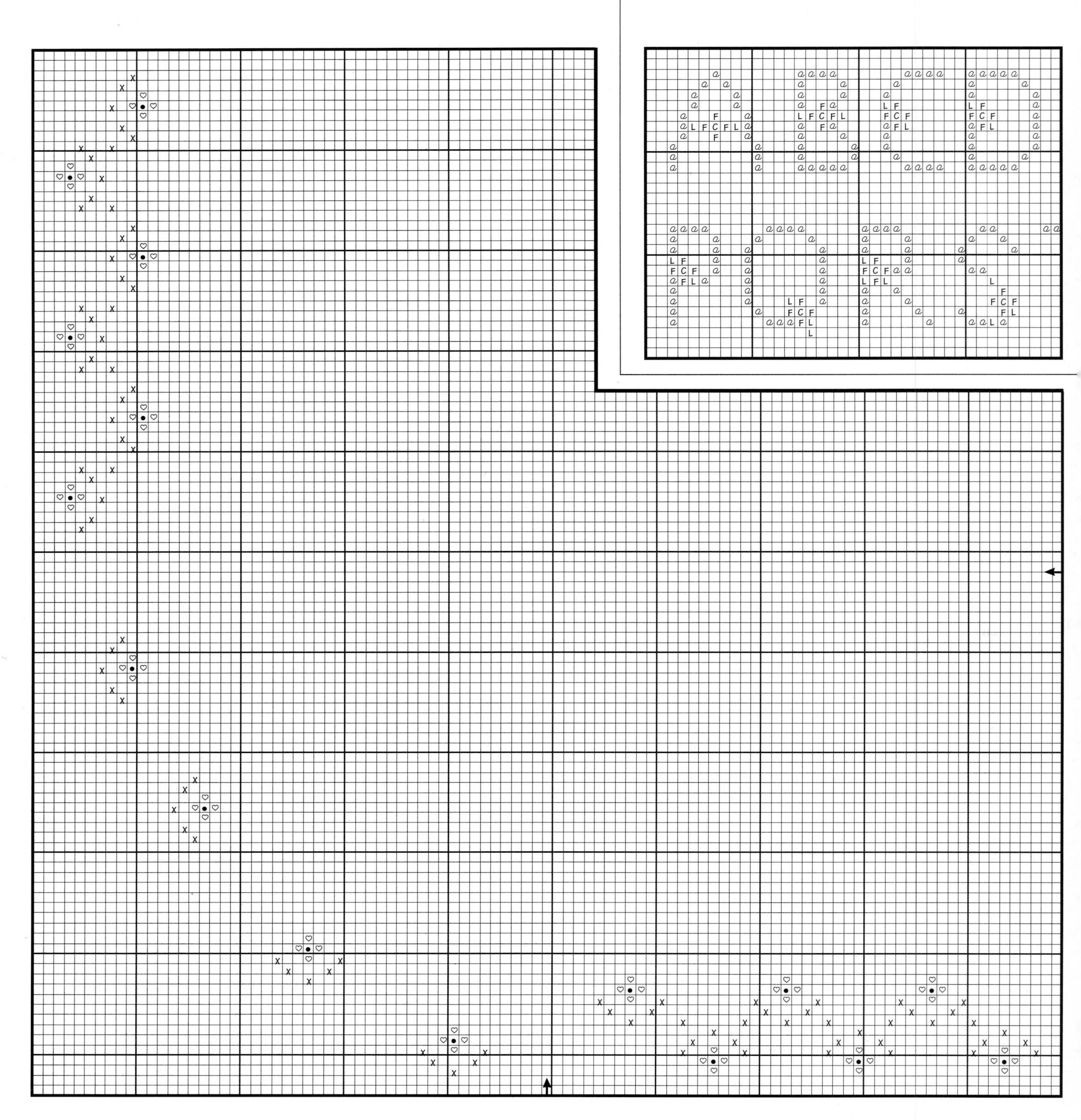

POSY BORDER

	DMC	COLOR
♡	761	salmon, lt.
•	727	topaz, vy. lt.
X	368	pistachio, lt.

Fabrics: ***Baby Blanket***—14-count yellow Soft Touch® Baby Blanket from Charles Craft, Inc.; ***Bottle Cover***—14-count white Aida insert on Baby Bottle Cover from The JanLynn® Corporation

Stitch count:

Posy Border	100H x 95W
Straight Portion	10H x 43W

Design size:

Posy Border	14-count	7⅛" x 6⅞"
Straight Portion	14-count	¾" x 3⅛"

Baby Blanket

Instructions: Cross stitch using three strands of floss. Stitch design 1" up binding on blanket.

Bottle Cover

Instructions: Cross stitch using three strands of floss. Center straight portion of design on cross-stitch fabric band of bottle cover and repeat motif as needed to go around bottle cover.

Shaded portion indicates overlap from previous page.

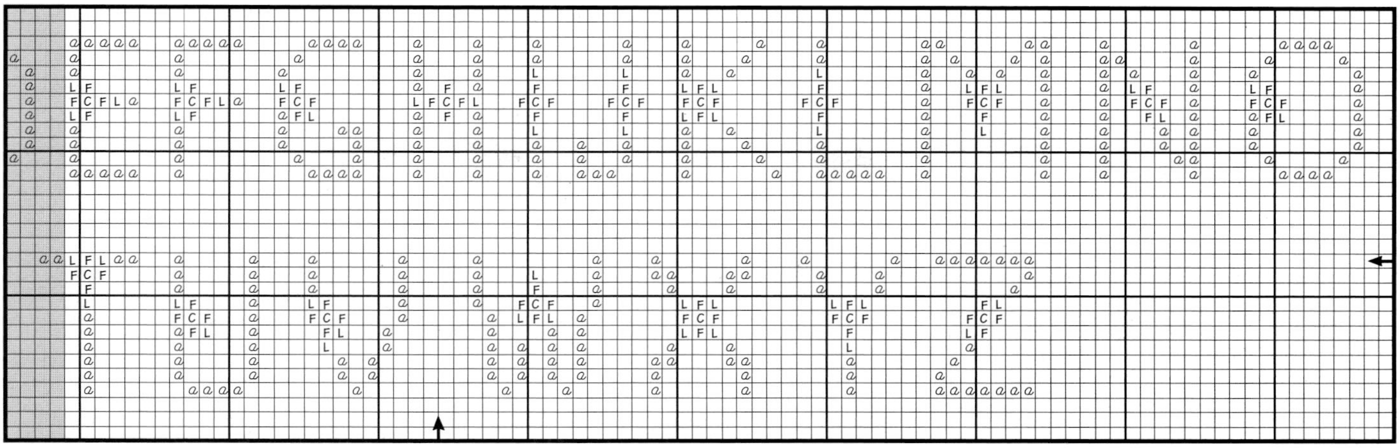

FLORAL ALPHABET

	DMC	COLOR
a	799	delft, med.
F	3689	mauve, lt.
C	727	topaz, vy. lt.
L	913	Nile green, med.

Fabrics: *Baby Blanket*—14-count blue Soft Touch® Baby Blanket from Charles Craft, Inc.; ***Socks***—27-count linen used as waste canvas

Stitch count:

A, M, W	10H x 9W
O	10H x 8W
D, K, N, R, T, V, X, Y, Z	10H x 7W
B, C, G, L, S, U	10H x 6W
E, F, H, J, P	10H x 5W
I	10H x 3W
Q	11H x 8W
Border	49H x 62W

Design size:

A, M, W	¾" x ⅝"
O	¾" x ⅝"
D, K, N, R, T, V, X, Y, Z	¾" x ½"
B, C, G, L, S, U	¾" x ½"
E, F, H, J, P	¾" x ⅜"
I	¾" x ¼"
Q	⅞" x ⅝"
Border	3½" x 4½"

Baby Blanket

Instructions: Cross stitch using three strands of floss. Stitch border 1½" up from binding. Place letters five squares above border design, leaving three spaces between each.

Socks

Instructions: Cross stitch over two threads using three strands of floss. Center letters 1" above lace-trimmed edge of cuff on outer side of sock.

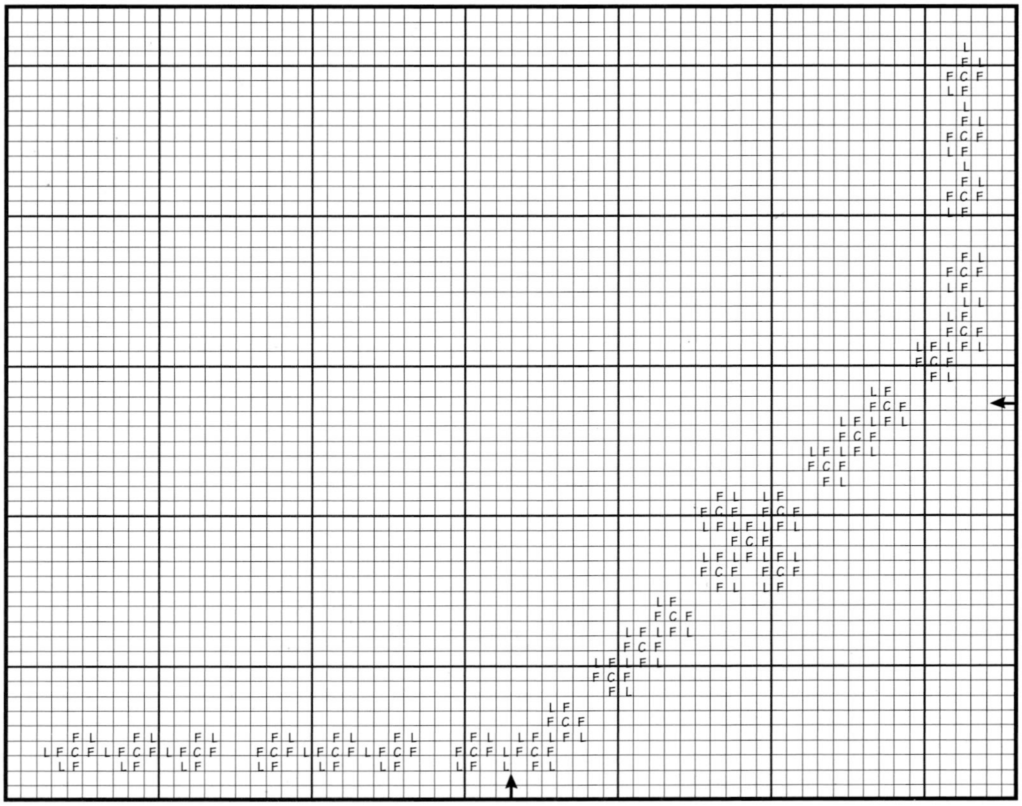

BORDER

Bug Alphabet

The tiny bug on each letter in this colorful *Bug Alphabet* is sure to tickle your youngster's fancy whether worked on a backpack, a shirt, or another favorite piece. Even little girls will like these whimsical "buggy" letters.

	DMC	COLOR
•	310	black
C	740	tangerine
ℓ	444	lemon, dk.
X	311	navy, med.
3	321	red
Δ	702	kelly green
P	975	gold-brown, dk.

Fabrics: ***Carry All***—14-count ivory Aida insert on navy Classic Carry All from The JanLynn® Corporation; ***Turtleneck and Book Bag***—20-count linen used as waste canvas

Stitch count:

M	13H x 13W
A, Z	13H x 12W
G, K, L, N, O, R, W, X	13H x 11W
B, V	13H x 10W
D, P, S	13H x 9W
H, T, U, Y	13H x 8W
C, E, F, J	13H x 7W
I	13H x 3W
Q	14H x 11W

Design size:

14-count

M	1" x 1"
A, Z	1" x ⅞"
G, K, L, N, O, R, W, X	1" x ⅞"
B, V	1" x ¾"
D, P, S	1" x ⅝"
H, T, U, Y	1" x ⅝"
C, E, F, J	1" x ½"
I	1" x ¼"
Q	1" x ⅞"

20-count

M	1⅜" x 1⅜"
A, Z	1⅜" x 1⅛"
G, K, L, N, O, R, W, X	1⅜" x 1⅛"
B, V	1⅜" x 1"
D, P, S	1⅜" x ⅞"
H, T, U, Y	1⅜" x ⅞"
C, E, F, J	1⅜" x ¾"
I	1⅜" x ⅜"
Q	1½" x 1⅛"

Carry All

Instructions: Cross stitch using three strands of floss. Backstitch using one strand of floss. Make French knots using two strands of floss, wrapping floss around needle once. Center letters on cross-stitch fabric panel.

Turtleneck and Book Bag

Instructions: Cross stitch over two threads using two strands of floss. Backstitch using one strand of floss. Make French knots using two strands of floss, wrapping floss around needle once. Center letters on front of turtleneck 2" down from neckline. Center letters on pocket of book bag.

Backstitch instructions:

702	frogs' toes on letters G, M, Z
321	snakes' tongues on letters F, P, T
310	all antennae, all legs

French knots instructions:

310	ends of all antennae, all spots on bugs

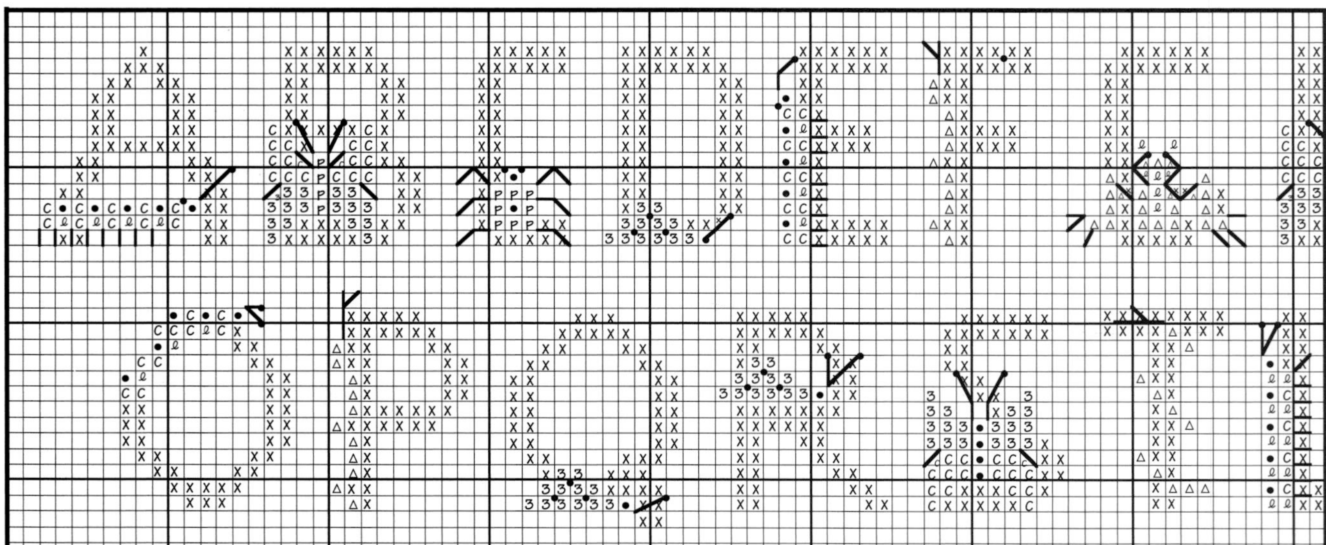

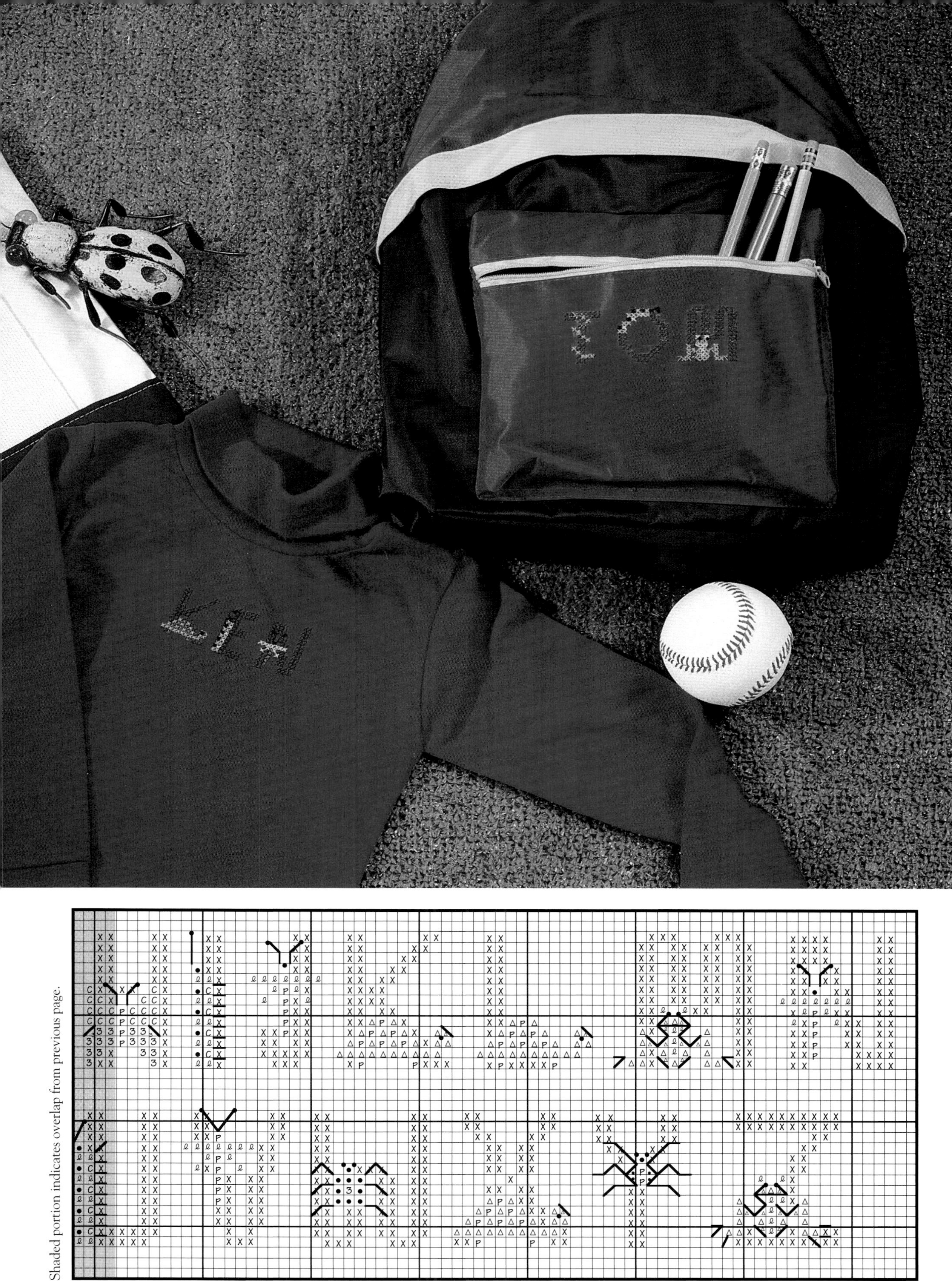

Shaded portion indicates overlap from previous page.

Balloons!

Colorful balloons captivate most any child's attention and bring warm smiles to young faces. Stitch a bunch of balloons on a sweatshirt for your child, gathering them with ribbon strings. A smiling teddy bear wearing diapers and holding a balloon in each paw will be ideal for your tot. An alphabet is included for personalization. Change the floss colors to match any outfit.

BEAR WITH BALLOONS

	DMC	COLOR
M	433	brown, med.
/	435	brown, vy. lt.
O	761	salmon, lt.
3	321	red
=	307	lemon
X	797	royal blue
6	700	green, bt.
■	310	black

Fabric: 27-count linen used as waste canvas on white sleeper
Stitch count: 25H x 19W
Design size:
27-count 1⅞" x 1⅜"

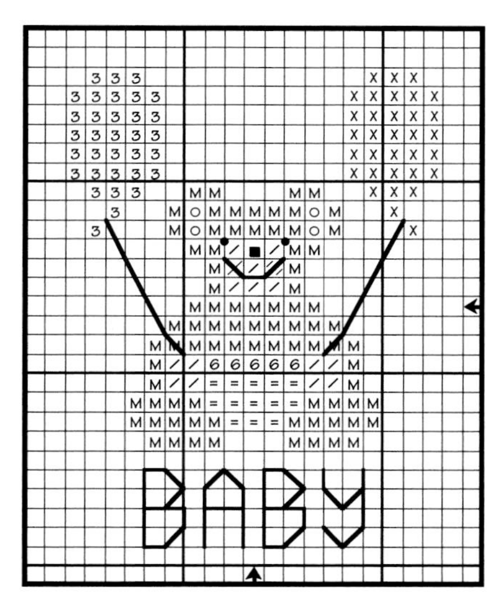

Instructions: Cross stitch over two threads using two strands of floss. Backstitch using one strand of floss unless otherwise indicated. Straight stitch for balloon strings using one strand of floss the color of balloon. Make French knots for eyes where ● appears at intersecting grid lines using two strands 310, wrapping floss around needle once.
NOTE: Use alphabet given to stitch name where *BABY* appears on chart.
Backstitch instructions:
310 mouth
700 lettering (two strands)

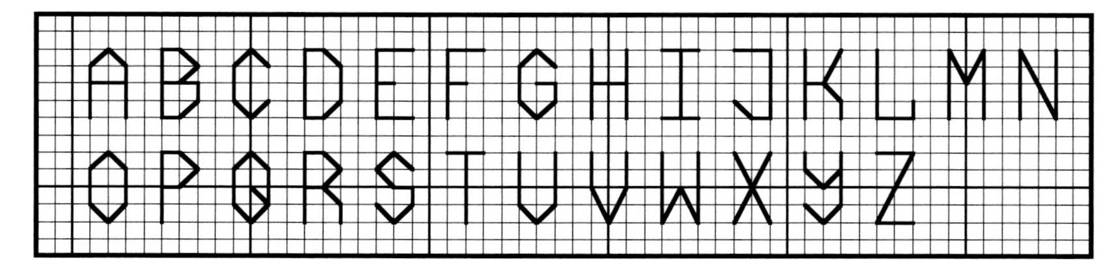

BRIGHT BALLOONS

	DMC	COLOR
–	444	lemon, dk.
C	666	red, bt.
X	996	electric blue, med.
●	white	white

Fabric: 20-count linen used as waste canvas on green sweatshirt
Stitch count: 49H x 30W
Design size:
20-count 5" x 3"

Instructions: Cross stitch over two threads using three strands of floss. Stitch design 1" in from left sleeve seam and 2" down from neckline.
NOTE: For balloon strings, cut three pieces of 1/16"-wide white satin ribbon, each 13" long. Tie a knot on one end of each piece and tack at the base of each balloon. Bring the free ends of ribbons together, tie in a knot, and tack to shirt.

Bunny "Tales"

An endearing bunny, complete with long ears and a fluffy tail, adorns these denim overalls, turning a ready-to-wear garment into custom-stitched fun. The delicate shades used to create our whiskered friend also make him suitable for infant clothing. Make him smaller or larger to fit the items he'll be on by varying the count of the waste canvas or fabric.

	DMC	Color
•	603	cranberry
X	604	cranberry, lt.
/	white	white

Fabrics: ***Denim Overalls and Mint Green Sleeper***—20-count linen used as waste canvas
Stitch count: 16H x 14W
Design size:
20-count 1⅝" x 1½"

Denim Overalls
Instructions: Cross stitch over two threads using four strands of floss. Straight stitch whiskers using two strands white. Center motif on top flap of overalls.

Mint Green Sleeper
Instructions: Cross stitch over two threads using four strands of floss. Straight stitch whiskers using two strands white. Stitch design on left side of sleeper 2" down from neckline.

Happy Clown

Capture the excitement of the circus—stitch our smiley-faced clown on a pair of boys' pajamas. Turn bedtime into a cheery occasion for your son or grandson as he wears his funny buddy to bed!

	DMC	COLOR
/	948	peach flesh, vy. lt.
W	3772	flesh, dk.
o	3326	rose, lt.
•	606	orange-red
✳	608	orange
+	444	lemon, dk.
3	797	royal blue
▲	701	green, lt.
–	white	white
■	310	black

Fabric: 20-count linen used as waste canvas on yellow sleeper
Stitch count: 20H x 14W
Design size:
20-count 2" x 1½"

Instructions: Cross stitch over two threads using four strands of floss. Backstitch using two strands of floss. Center design on left side of sleeper 2" down from shoulder seam.
Backstitch instructions:
310 eyes, mouth
701 flower stem

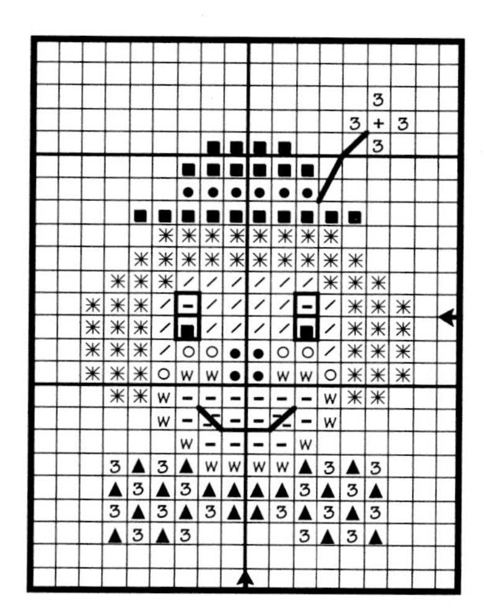

Pinwheel Bouquet

Looking for a quick-to-finish shower gift? The *Pinwheel Bouquet*, stitched on a pink sleeper, will be a pleasing present for a baby girl! For use in the nursery, work the design on Ribband® and fashion a decorative bow for trimming a small basket filled with baby supplies.

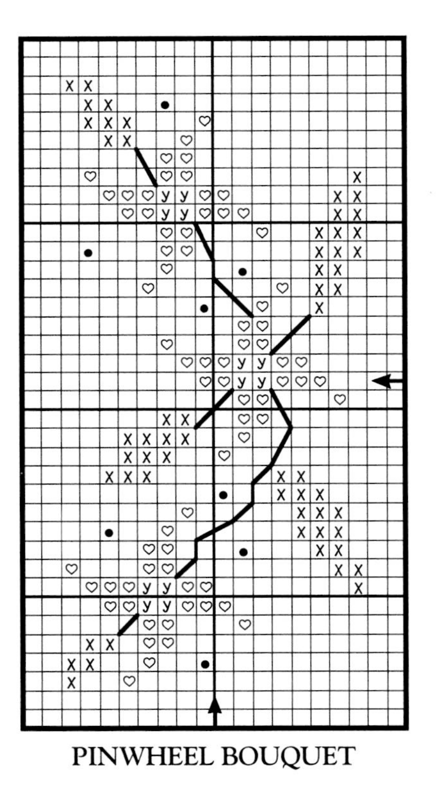

PINWHEEL BOUQUET

	DMC	COLOR
X	502	blue-green
♡	961	dusty rose, dk.
y	676	old gold, lt.
•	500	blue-green, vy. dk.

Fabrics: ***Sleeper***—28-count linen used as waste canvas; ***Bow***—18-count Aida Ribband® with green trim from Leisure Arts

Stitch count:

Pinwheel Bouquet	33H x 16W
Flower	10H x 10W

Design size:

Pinwheel Bouquet	28-count	2⅜" x 1⅛"
	18-count	1⅞" x ⅞"
Flower	28-count	¾" x ¾"
	18-count	⅝" x ⅝"

Sleeper
Instructions: Cross stitch over two threads using two strands of floss. Backstitch using one strand 500. Center *Pinwheel Bouquet* between snaps on front placket. Center *Flower* on each sleeve ¾" up from edge of sleeve, directly across from sleeve seam.

Bow
Instructions: Cross stitch using two strands of floss. Backstitch using one strand 500. Center *Pinwheel Bouquet* sideways on Ribband® and stitch twice, leaving 2" between designs. Center *Flower* sideways on Ribband® and stitch once. Finishing instructions are on page 142.

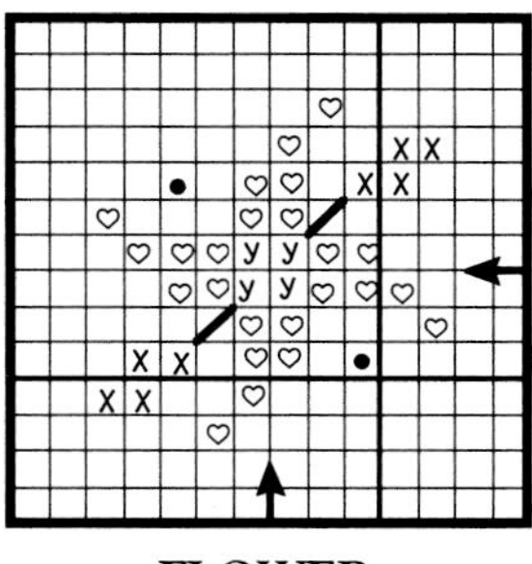

FLOWER

ABC Blocks

A bright yellow sweat suit forms an ideal background for the *ABC Blocks* designs. Worked here across the top, the blocks can also be placed on the back or even on the sleeves. Complete the ensemble by working a block or two on the sweatpants, and you will have an outfit your youngster will want to wear every day.

	DMC	COLOR
•	321	red
■	310	black
//	white	white
○	970	pumpkin, lt.
=	899	rose, med.
6	434	brown, lt.
ǀ	738	tan, vy. lt.
L	754	peach flesh, lt.
●	702	kelly green
▲	825	blue, dk.
\	444	lemon, dk.

Fabric: 27-count linen used as waste canvas on yellow sweatsuit

Stitch count:

Six Blocks	34H x 54W
Two Blocks	34H x 14W

Design size:

Six Blocks	27-count	2½" x 4"
Two Blocks	27-count	2½" x 1⅛"

Instructions: Cross stitch over two threads using two strands of floss. Backstitch using two strands of floss. Make French knot for bear's nose where • appears at intersecting grid lines using two strands 310, wrapping floss around needle once. Center *Six Blocks* on shirt 2" below neckline. Place *Two Blocks* on left thigh of pants 9" below waistband.

Backstitch instructions:

310	bear's smile
321	clown's smile
434	apple stem

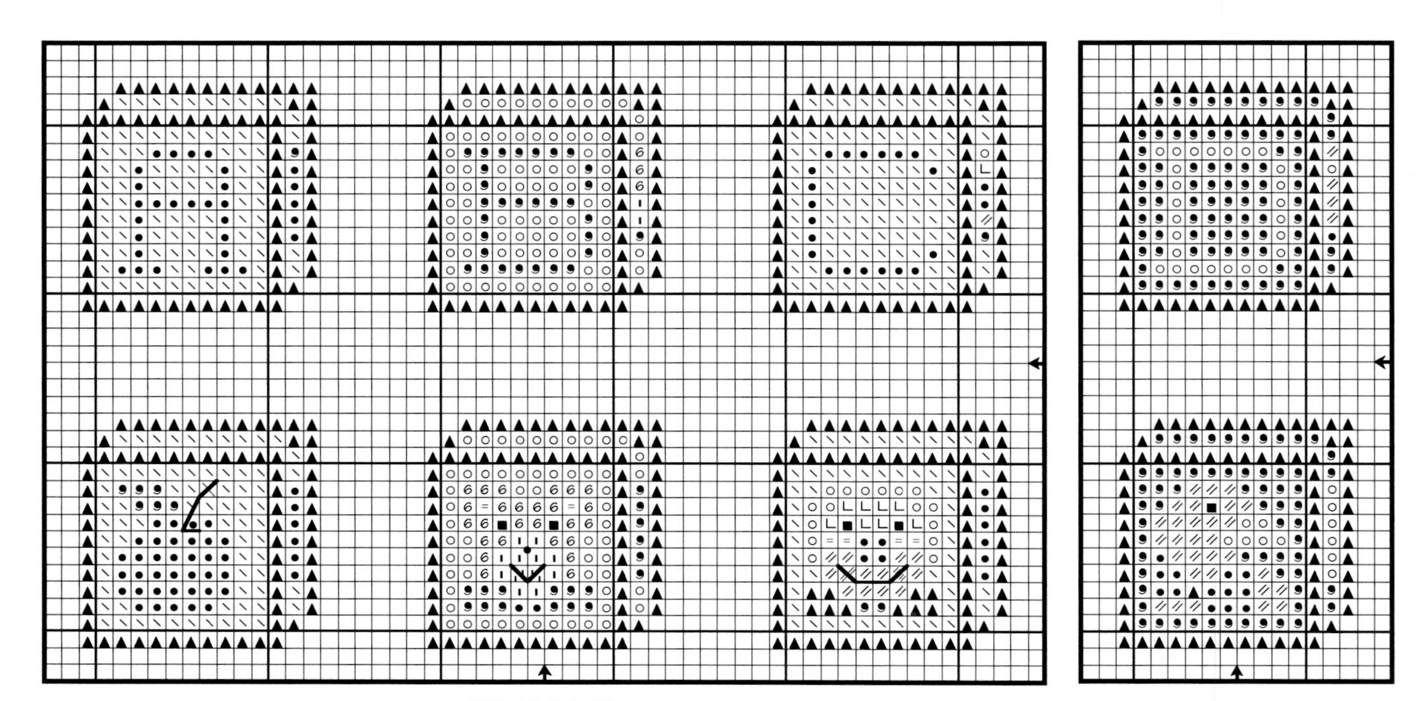

SIX BLOCKS

TWO BLOCKS

Fancy Flowers

Transform a purchased velvet dress into an heirloom for a little darling of yours by trimming the collar with the meandering *Floral Border* design. Every young princess will love having this keepsake dress to wear! For everyday wear, stitch the dainty *Forget-me-not Bouquet* on a ready-made knit dress. Chart for *Forget-me-not Bouquet* is on page 15.

FLORAL BORDER

	DMC	COLOR
o	3689	mauve, lt.
ℓ	3685	mauve, dk.
#	3348	yellow-green, lt.

Fabric: 27-count linen used as waste canvas on white collar of velvet dress

Stitch count:

Center Border	27H x 27W
Side Border	7H x 50W

Design size:

Center Border	27-count	2" x 2"
Side Border	27-count	⅝" x 3¾"

Instructions: Cross stitch over two threads using two strands of floss. Backstitch using one strand 3348. Center point of *Center Border* ½" from collar edge. Stitch *Side Border* on both sides of *Center Border*, leaving ½" between *Center Border* and *Side Border*.

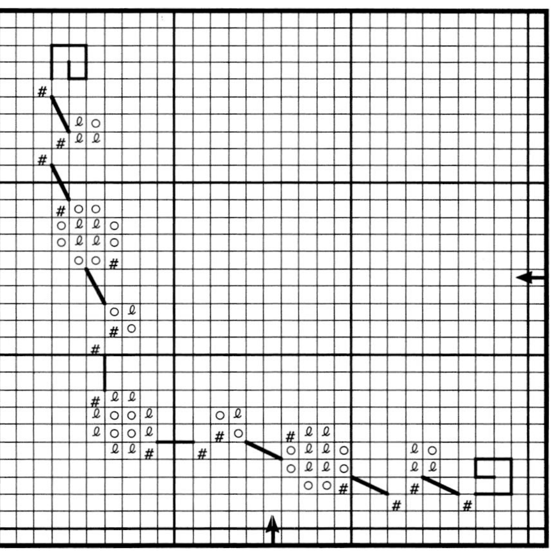

CENTER BORDER

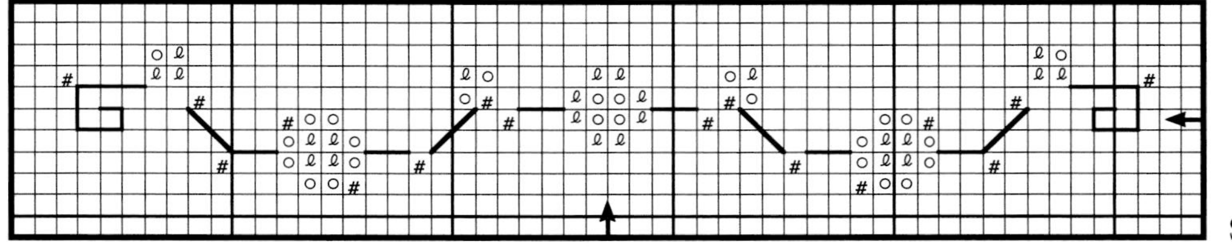

SIDE BORDER

For the Kitchen

Add a personal touch to your kitchen's decor. Stitched accents worked on place mats, napkins, and other accessories complement the room whether it's comfortably casual or decidedly formal. These designs are suitable for items from plain to fancy, and the time you spend cooking will be especially enjoyable when you're surrounded by your handiwork.

Miniature Houses

These charming little houses, stitched individually or all in a row, will make an inviting collection when they're worked on place mats, napkins, and bread covers. If your time permits, choose an alphabet from those included throughout these pages and add a monogram or name under the houses. These tiny dwellings can also be custom-colored to match your home and will be darling worked on a blouse collar!

	DMC	COLOR
▲	930	antique blue, dk.
3	931	antique blue, med.
⟍	932	antique blue, lt.
e	3777	terra cotta, vy. dk.
II	ecru	ecru
■	310	black
•	413	pewter gray, dk.
6	935	avocado, dk.
V	3051	green-gray, dk.
C	3052	green-gray, med.
X	301	mahogany, med.
L	437	tan, lt.
O	676	old gold, lt.
✱	898	coffee brown, vy. dk.
/	415	pearl gray
Z	433	brown, med.
⟀	414	steel gray, dk.
=	3046	yellow-beige, med.
I	677	old gold, vy. lt.
W	355	terra cotta, dk.
W	356	terra cotta, med.
◣	355	terra cotta, dk.
●	400	mahogany, dk.
4	435	brown, vy. lt.
▼	3371	black-brown

Fabrics: ***Table Linens***—26-count white fringed place mat, napkin, and bread cover from Carolina Cross Stitch; ***Pillowcase***—28-count linen used as waste canvas

(Color code and charts continue on page 64.)

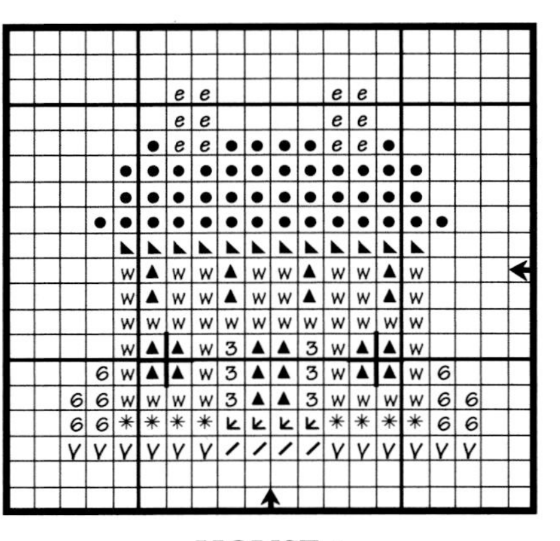

HOUSE 1

HOUSE 2

HOUSE 3

CRABTREE
INGREDIENTS

Stitch count:

House 1	15H x 16W
House 2	14H x 18W
House 3	14H x 20W
House 4	14H x 19W
House 5	15H x 19W
House 6	17H x 15W
House 7	13H x 20W
House 8	17H x 16W
House 9	12H x 21W

Design size:

House 1	26-count	1⅛" x 1¼"
	28-count	1⅛" x 1⅛"
House 2	26-count	1⅛" x 1⅜"
House 3	26-count	1⅛" x 1⅝"
	28-count	1" x 1½"
House 4	26-count	1" x 1½"
House 5	26-count	1⅛" x 1½"
	28-count	1⅛" x 1⅜"
House 6	26-count	1⅜" x 1⅛"
	28-count	1¼" x 1⅛"
House 7	26-count	1" x 1⅝"
House 8	26-count	1⅜" x 1¼"
House 9	26-count	1" x 1⅝"
	28-count	⅞" x 1½"

Table Linens (Photo is on pages 62–63.)
Instructions: Cross stitch over two threads using two strands of floss. Backstitch using one strand of floss. When two colors are bracketed together, use one strand of each.

Place Mat— Center *House 4* 1" down from fringed edge of place mat. Stitch *House 1* and *House 2* on left side of *House 4*, leaving 2" between designs. Stitch *House 7* and *House 9* on right side of *House 4*, leaving 2" between designs.
Napkins—Stitch *House 3* or *House 5* in lower left corner ½" from fabric edges.
Bread Cover—Stitch *House 8* in lower left corner ½" up from lower fabric edge and 1½" in from left fabric edge. Turn fabric ¼-turn counterclockwise and stitch *House 6* in lower right corner ½" up from lower fabric edge and 1½" in from right fabric edge.

Pillowcase (Photo is on page 87.)
Instructions: Cross stitch over two threads using two strands of floss. Backstitch using one strand of floss. Center *House 6* on pillowcase band. Stitch *House 3* and *House 9* on left side of *House 6*, leaving six threads between designs. Stitch *House 5* and *House 1* on right side of *House 6*, leaving six threads between designs.

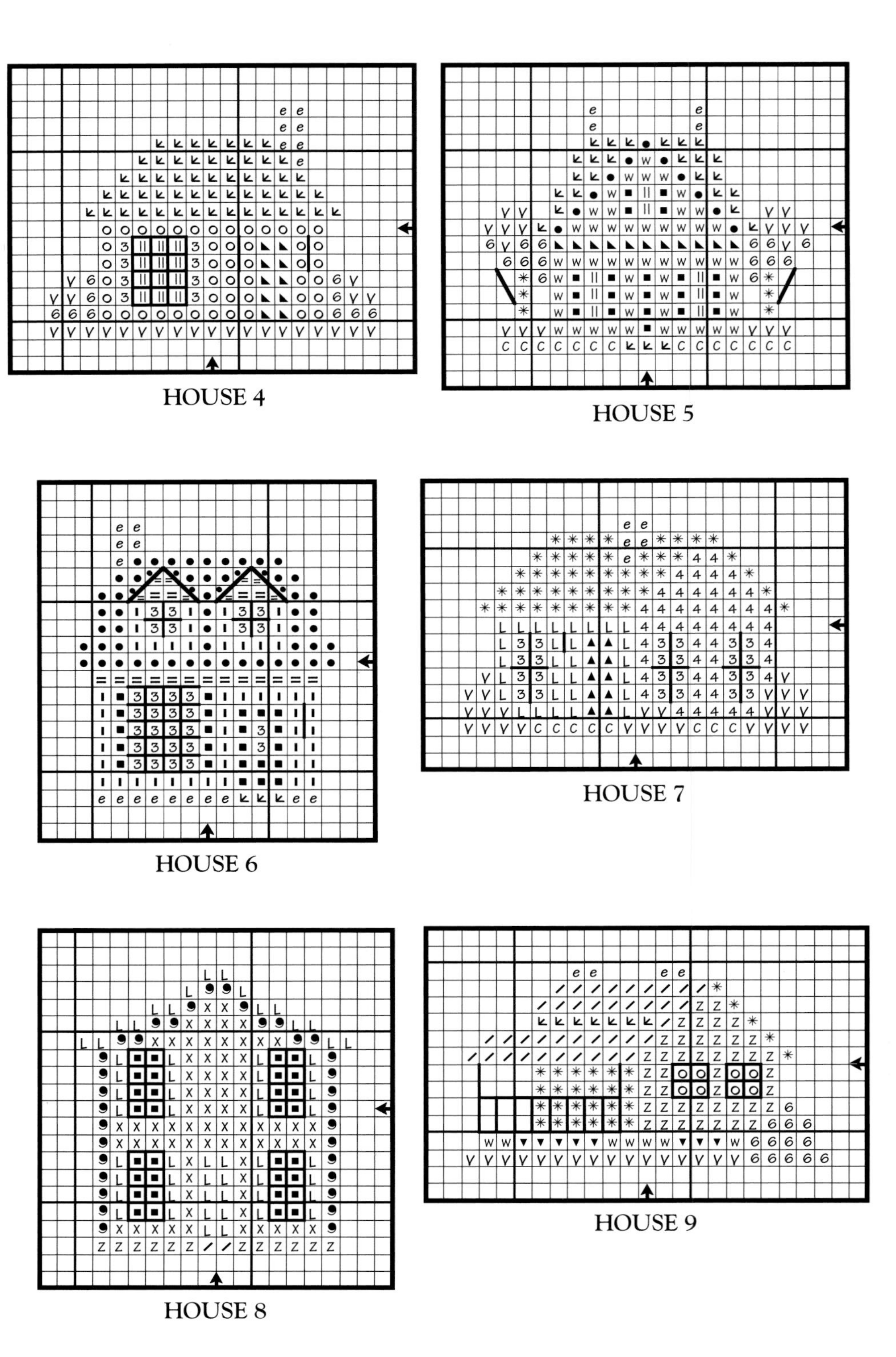

HOUSE 4

HOUSE 5

HOUSE 6

HOUSE 7

HOUSE 8

HOUSE 9

Backstitch instructions:

415	windowpanes in *House 1*
898	windowpanes in *House 2*, branches in *House 3*, branches in *House 5*, windowpanes and light beside door in *House 7*
676	windowpanes in *House 3*
930	windowpanes and lights beside front door in *House 4*
310	gables and light beside door in *House 6*
413	windowpanes in *House 6*
437	windowpanes in *House 8*
3371	porch and windows in *House 9*

Tea Party

Every woman longs for a spot of leisure time each day to sip tea; and some ladies collect vintage cups, saucers, and teapots just for this late-afternoon occasion. Let this fringed towel, embellished with necessities for teatime, be a stitched tribute to the tea sets that have been lovingly handed down from one generation to another.

	DMC	COLOR
•	336	navy
X	932	antique blue, lt.
♡	3328	salmon, med.
S	648	beaver gray, lt.

Fabrics: ***Tea Towel***—14-count cream tea towel from Carolina Cross Stitch, Inc.; ***Mini Tote***—20-count linen used as waste canvas on Mini Tote from The JanLynn® Corporation

Stitch count:

Tea Set	25H x 59W
Teapot	18H x 28W

Design size:

Tea Set	14-count	1¾" x 4¼"
Teapot	20-count	1⅞" x 2⅞"

Tea Towel

Instructions: Cross stitch using three strands of floss. Backstitch using two strands 336. Center design 1" up from lower fabric edge.

Mini Tote (Photo is on page 103.)

Instructions: Cross stitch over two threads using two strands of floss. Backstitch using one strand 336. Center teapot on side of tote 1" down from top fabric edge.

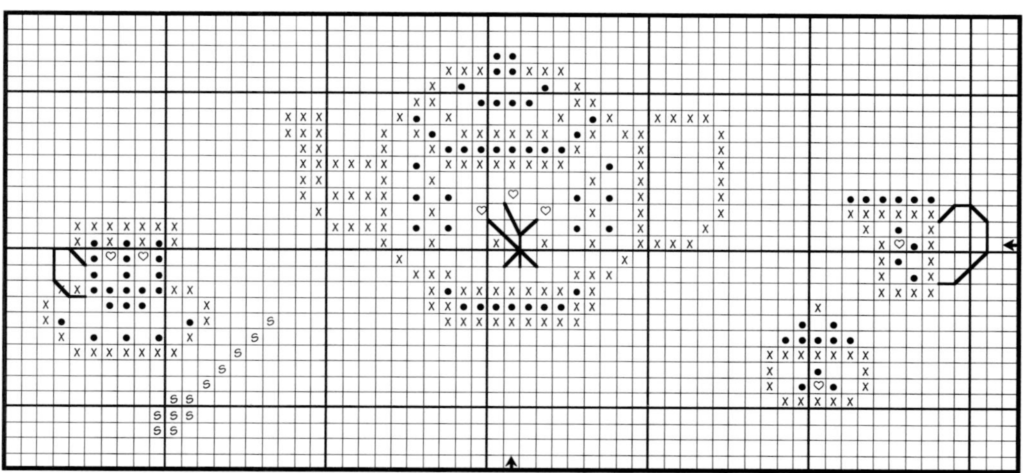

Tulips and Hearts

Warm rose and country blue hues form pretty hearts and flowers atop this cleverly finished mug coaster. Taking its cue from traditional surface protectors, this practical device will shield your furniture from hot

cups in a very fashionable manner. What a wonderful way to show off your handiwork! The tulips and hearts have also been worked side by side across the border of a cross-stitch terry towel to complete the duo.

	DMC	COLOR
•	930	antique blue, dk.
X	931	antique blue, med.
C	932	antique blue, lt.
▲	221	pink, dk.
3	223	pink, med.
/	224	pink, lt.
●	315	mauve, dk.
O	316	mauve, med.
–	3727	mauve, lt.
W	367	pistachio, dk.

Fabrics: ***Mug Coaster***—27-count off-white linen from Norden Crafts; ***Towel***—14-count blue mist Checked Cafe Towel from Charles Craft, Inc.

Stitch count:
Mug Coaster 50H x 50W
Towel 20H x 180W

Design size:
Mug Coaster 3¾" x 3¾"
Towel 1½" x 12⅞"

Mug Coaster

Instructions: Cross stitch over two threads using two strands of floss. Backstitch tulip stems using two strands 367. Make French knot where • appears at intersecting grid lines using two strands 221, wrapping floss around needle once. Finishing instructions are on page 142.

Towel

Instructions: Cross stitch using two strands of floss. Backstitch tulip stems using two strands 367. Make French knot where • appears at intersecting grid lines using two strands 221, wrapping floss around needle once. Beginning on left side of towel, stitch motifs side by side in the following order: 1, 4, 2, 3, 1, 3, 2, 4, 1. Do not leave any spaces between motifs.

Mini Fruits

Kitchens have been decorated with items containing a variety of fruit designs for many years; and with the recent trends in wallpaper and china, fruit is here to stay in an assortment of "tasteful" accessories. These stitched "edibles" will provide a great way to include this popular style in your decor whether they're presented by themselves or in selected groups. Looking for something a bit out of the ordinary? Work a different single motif on each piece of several matching place mat and napkin sets and mix and match them for a fantastic start to an unforgettable table!

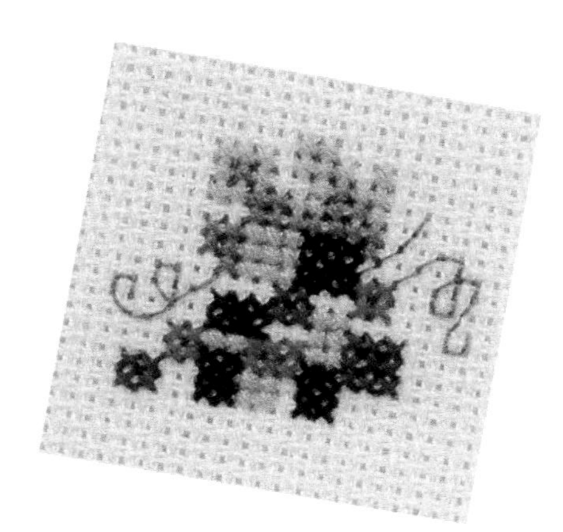

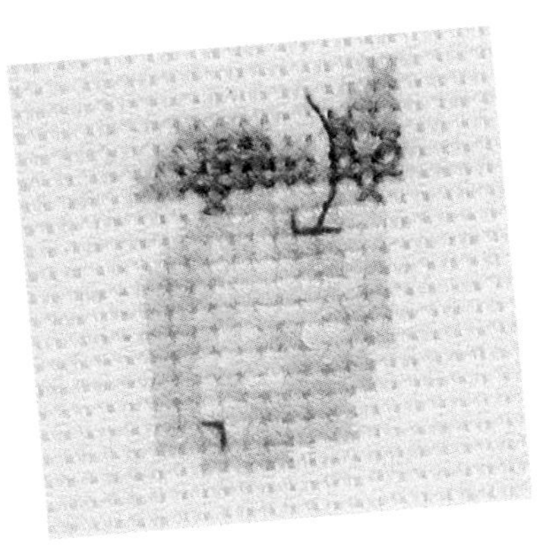

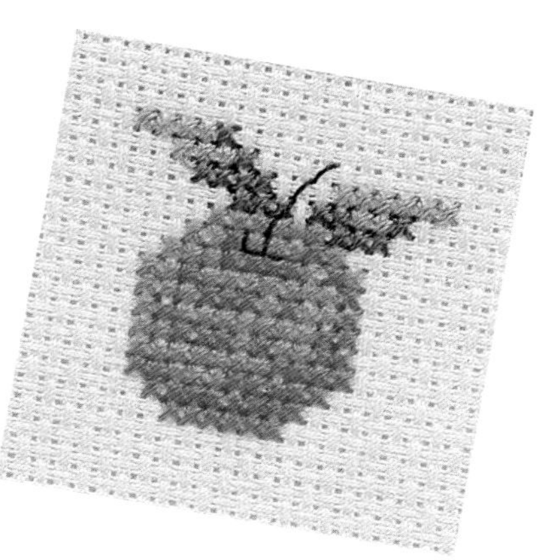

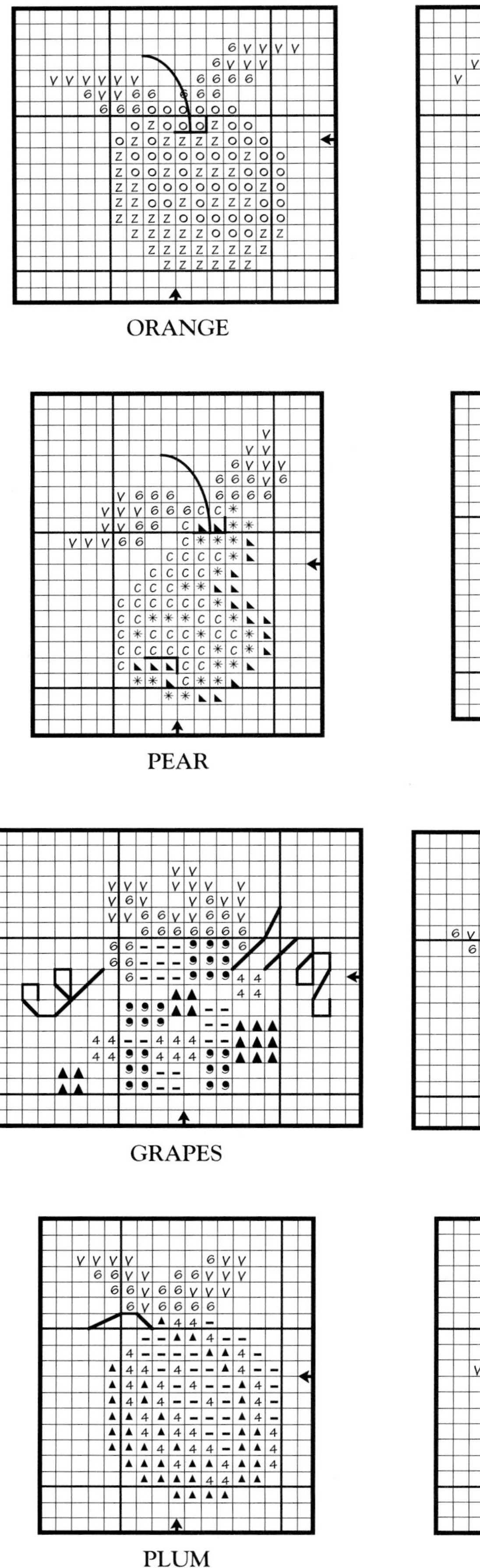

ORANGE

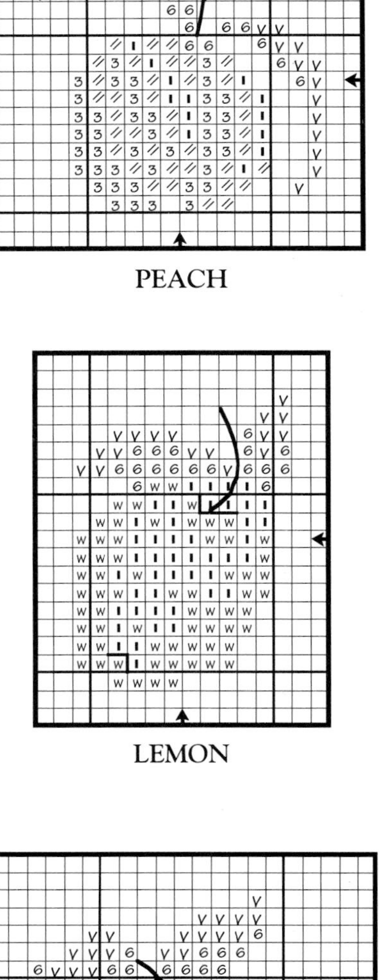

PEACH

PEAR

LEMON

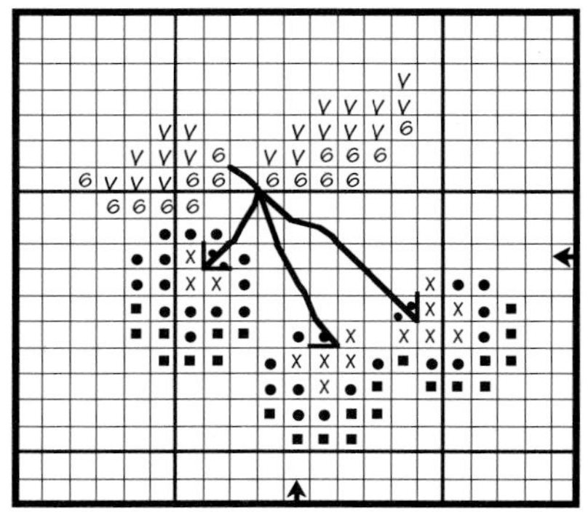

GRAPES

CHERRIES

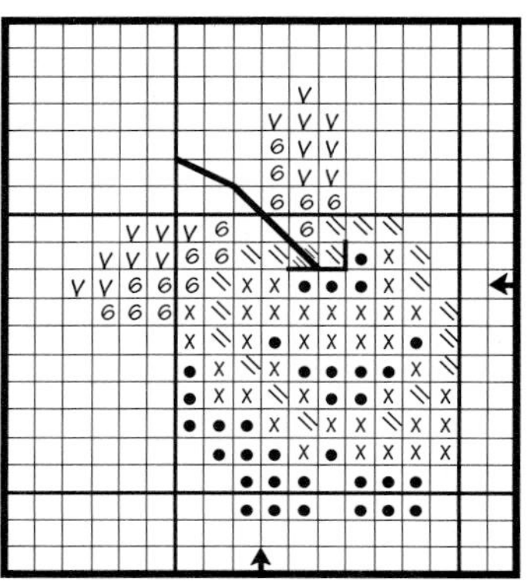

PLUM

APPLE

MINI FRUITS

	DMC	COLOR
6	469	avocado
V	471	avocado, vy. lt.
•	815	garnet, med.
X	498	red, dk.
3	722	spice, lt.
//	3341	apricot
✳	832	olive
C	833	olive, lt.
Z	740	tangerine
O	741	tangerine, med.
■	814	garnet, dk.
W	725	topaz
I	727	topaz, vy. lt.
▲	550	violet, vy. dk.
4	552	violet, med.
◣	829	olive, vy. dk.
●	823	navy, dk.
–	554	violet, lt.
⑊	321	red
bs	898	coffee brown, vy. dk.

Fabrics: ***Pot Holder***—14-count ecru KitchenMate pot holder from Charles Craft, Inc.; ***Ecru Towel***—14-count ecru KitchenMate terry towel from Charles Craft, Inc.; ***White Towel***—14-count white Fingertips™ towel with banana ice trim from Charles Craft, Inc.

Stitch count:

Orange	15H x 16W
Peach	15H x 16W
Pear	18H x 14W
Lemon	17H x 12W
Grapes	15H x 19W
Cherries	15H x 17W
Plum	16H x 13W
Apple	16H x 14W

Design size:
14-count

Orange	1⅛" x 1⅛"
Peach	1⅛" x 1⅛"
Pear	1¼" x 1"
Lemon	1¼" x ⅞"
Grapes	1⅛" x 1⅜"
Cherries	1⅛" x 1¼"
Plum	1⅛" x 1"
Apple	1⅛" x 1"

Instructions: Cross stitch using two strands of floss. Backstitch using one strand of floss.
Pot Holder—Stitch *Apple* on left side of cross-stitch fabric band four squares in and four squares down from fabric edges. Then stitch *Peach*, *Orange*, and *Pear* designs, leaving ten squares between each.
Ecru Towel— Center *Grapes* on cross-stitch fabric panel. Repeat design on either side, leaving ten squares between each.
White Towel—Center *Lemon* on cross-stitch fabric panel. Stitch *Cherries* on left side and *Plum* on right side, leaving ten squares between designs.

Backstitch (bs) instructions:

469	tendrils on *Grapes*
898	remainder of backstitching

Pear Tree

Don't look for partridges in this pear tree. But do stitch the *Pear Tree* design on purchased place mats and napkins to make interesting table accessories. When the mats are made of materials that are difficult to embroider, simply decorate the matching cloth napkins and fold them to show your work.

	DMC	COLOR
•	801	coffee, dk.
X	435	brown, vy. lt.
6	500	blue-green, vy. dk.

Fabric: 27-count linen used as waste canvas on light green napkins
Stitch count: 23H x 20W
Design size:
27-count 1¾" x 1½"

Instructions: Cross stitch over two threads using two strands of floss. Backstitch pears using one strand 435. Stitch design in lower-right corner of napkin 1" from fabric edges.

Veggies

The vivid colors of these ripe vegetables bring to mind the appetizing aromas of summer stews and soups—memories of picking the bounty from the garden and canning at Grandma's house. Stitch these veggies on cloth table accents, aprons, and other kitchen accessory items. Present them to your mother or grandmother and delight in the fond recollections they stir.

VEGGIES

	DMC	COLOR
S	701	green, lt.
P	550	violet, vy. dk.
d	327	violet, dk.
o	3078	golden yellow, vy. lt.
•	895	green, dk.
ø	970	pumpkin, lt.
⁙	437	tan, lt.
a	321	red
X	369	pistachio, vy. lt.
H	610	drab brown, vy. dk.
3	368	pistachio, lt.
\\	744	yellow, pl.
>	209	lavender, dk.
◐	814	garnet, dk.
I	white	white

Fabrics: ***Apron***—26-count cream apron with lace trim from Carolina Cross Stitch, Inc.; ***Oven Mitt***—14-count buttered almond KitchenMates oven mitt from Charles Craft, Inc.; ***Napkins***—20-count linen used as waste canvas on blue napkins

Stitch count:

Turnip	11H x 12W
Beets	19H x 21W
Green Onions	23H x 13W
English Peas	8H x 20W
Yellow Onion	15H x 13W
Cabbage	13H x 16W
Squash	13H x 20W
Tomato	13H x 15W
Bell Peppers	13H x 16W
Broccoli	12H x 20W
Cauliflower	11H x 14W
Eggplant	17H x 10W
Radishes	16H x 19W
Carrots	18H x 23W
Celery	25H x 10W
Asparagus	20H x 8W
Corn	25H x 21W

Design size:

Turnip	26-count	⅞" x 1"
Beets	26-count	1½" x 1⅝"
	20-count	2" x 2⅛"
Green Onions	26-count	1¾" x 1"
English Peas	26-count	⅝" x 1⅝"
Yellow Onion	26-count	1⅛" x 1"
Cabbage	26-count	1" x 1¼"
Squash	26-count	1" x 1⅝"
Tomato	26-count	1" x 1⅛"
	14-count	1" x 1⅛"
Bell Peppers	26-count	1" x 1¼"
	14-count	1" x 1⅛"
Broccoli	26-count	1" x 1⅝"
	14-count	⅞" x 1½"
Cauliflower	26-count	⅞" x 1⅛"
Eggplant	26-count	1⅜" x ¾"
Radishes	26-count	1¼" x 1½"
	20-count	1⅝" x 2"
Carrots	26-count	1⅜" x 1¾"
Celery	26-count	2" x ¾"
Asparagus	26-count	1⅝" x ⅝"
Corn	26-count	2" x 1⅝"

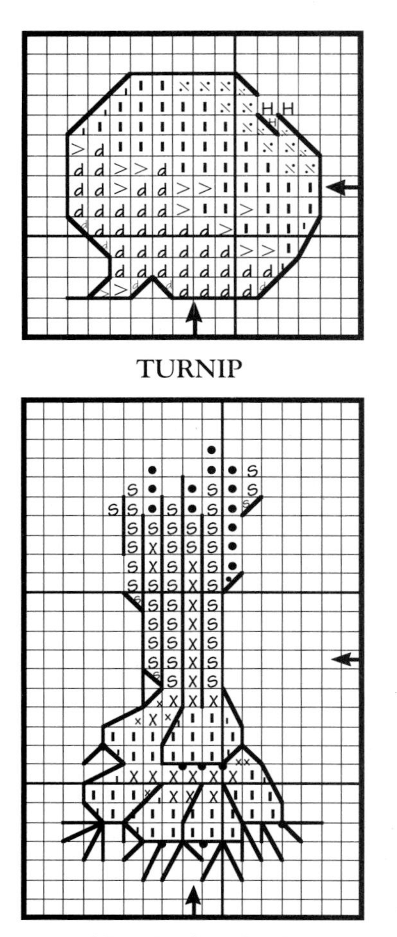

TURNIP

GREEN ONIONS

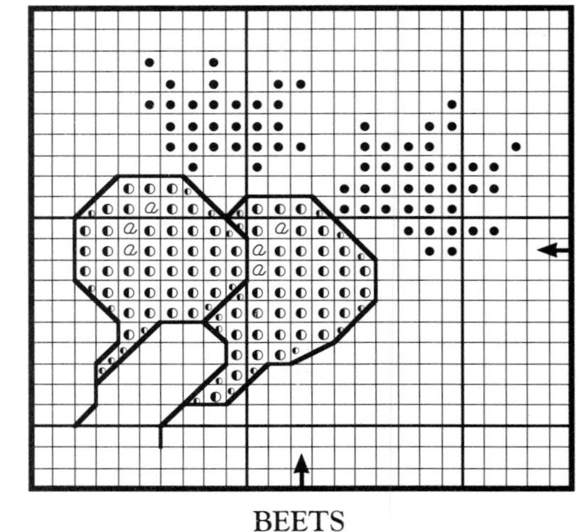

BEETS

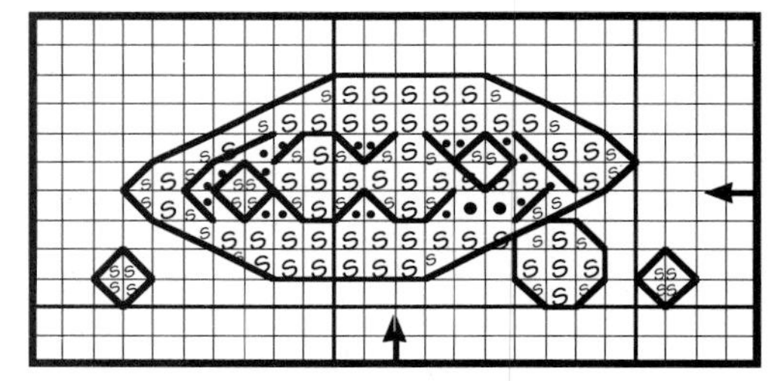

ENGLISH PEAS

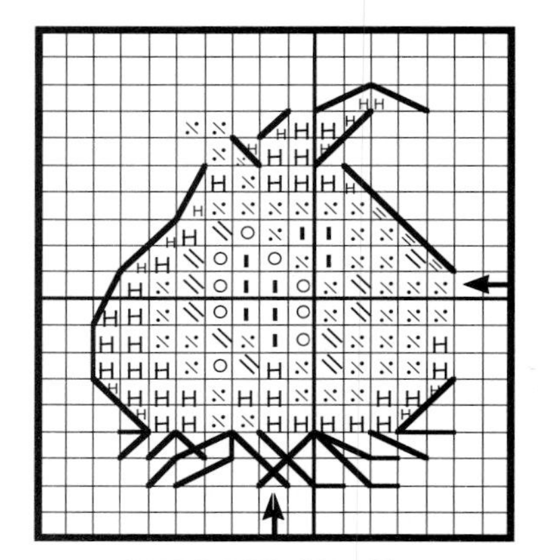

YELLOW ONION

Apron

Instructions: Cross stitch over two threads using two strands of floss. Backstitch using one strand of floss. Stitch designs ½" from fabric edges, leaving 1¼" between each.

Oven Mitt

Instructions: Cross stitch using two strands of floss. Backstitch using one strand of floss. Stitch *Tomato* in upper-right corner ¾" from cross-stitch fabric edges. Stitch *Broccoli* in upper-left corner 1" from cross-stitch fabric edges. Center *Bell Peppers* ½" up from lower edge of cross-stitch fabric.

Napkins (Shown as napkin and bread cover.)

Instructions: Cross stitch over two threads using two strands of floss. Backstitch using one strand of floss. Stitch designs in lower-left corner 1" from fabric edges.

Backstitch instructions:

701	lower leaves in *Cauliflower*, stems in *Carrots*
970	orange areas in *Carrots*
368	remainder of backstitching in *Cauliflower*
437	silks in *Corn*, roots in *Green Onions*, all backstitching in *Squash*, spears in *Asparagus*
321	all backstitching in *Tomato*
895	all backstitching in *English Peas*, all backstitching in *Celery*, bulbs and leaves in *Green Onions*, green areas of *Bell Peppers*, stem in *Broccoli*, all backstitching in *Cabbage*
550	garnet areas in *Radishes*, all backstitching in *Turnip*, all backstitching in *Beets*
610	roots in *Yellow Onion*
327	purple areas in *Eggplant*
814	red areas in *Bell Peppers*, red and white areas in *Radishes*
369	lower edge in *Asparagus*

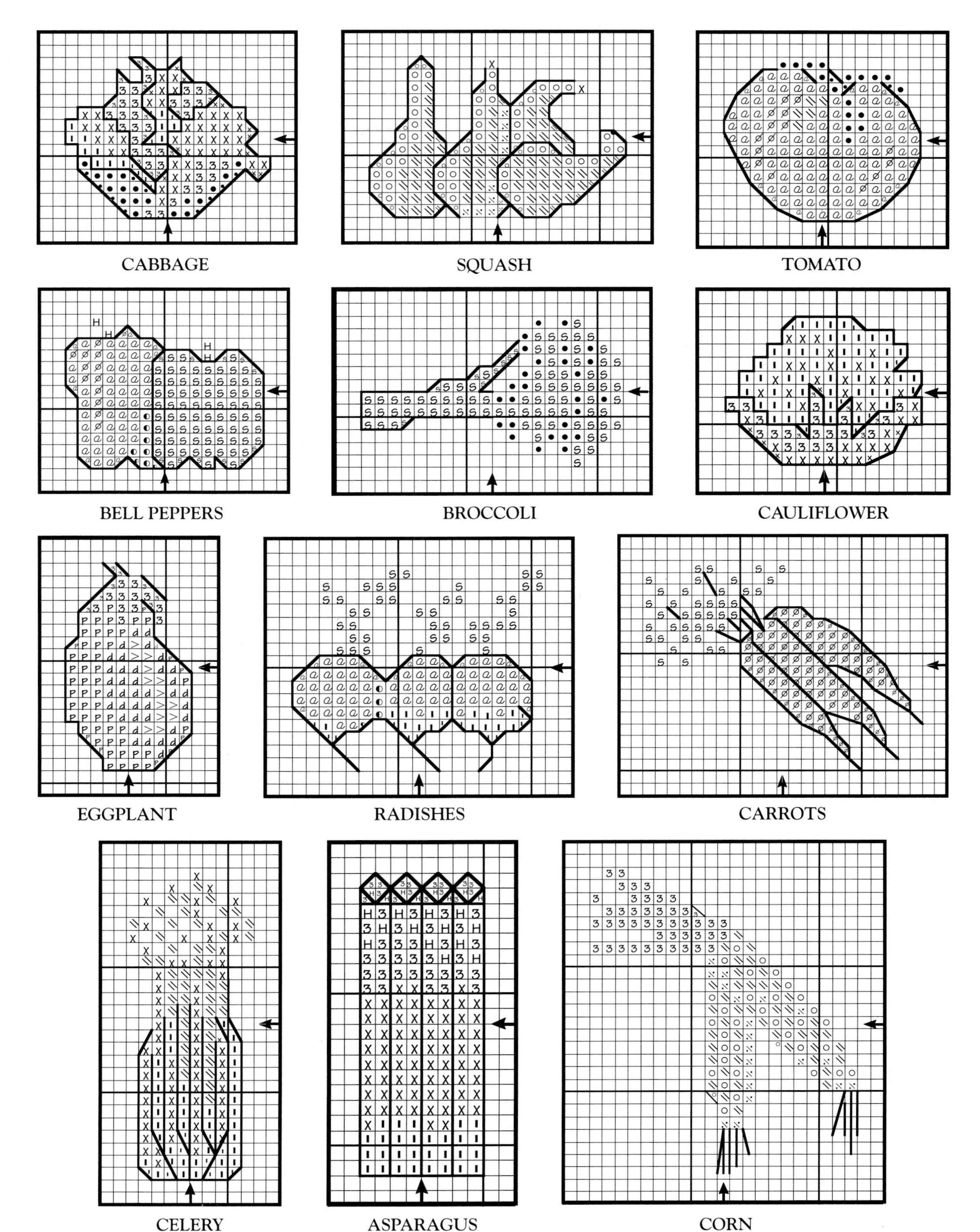
CABBAGE
SQUASH
TOMATO
BELL PEPPERS
BROCCOLI
CAULIFLOWER
EGGPLANT
RADISHES
CARROTS
CORN

CELERY

ASPARAGUS

Magnet Trio

The refrigerator door has become the message center of the house, the showcase for important schoolwork, and an ideal spot for personal tips. When those tips come in the form of cross-stitch pieces popped into refrigerator magnets, they're certain to bring a smile even if the hint they send is a bit on the serious side. *Eat Smart* and *Health Is True Wealth* can be used as helpful reminders for those folks who need occasional encouragement when it comes to sticking with wholesome foods. *Eat Dessert First* carries "flavorful" appeal for dieters and non-dieters alike; and if you tend to be self-indulgent, you'd better watch out for this stitchery!

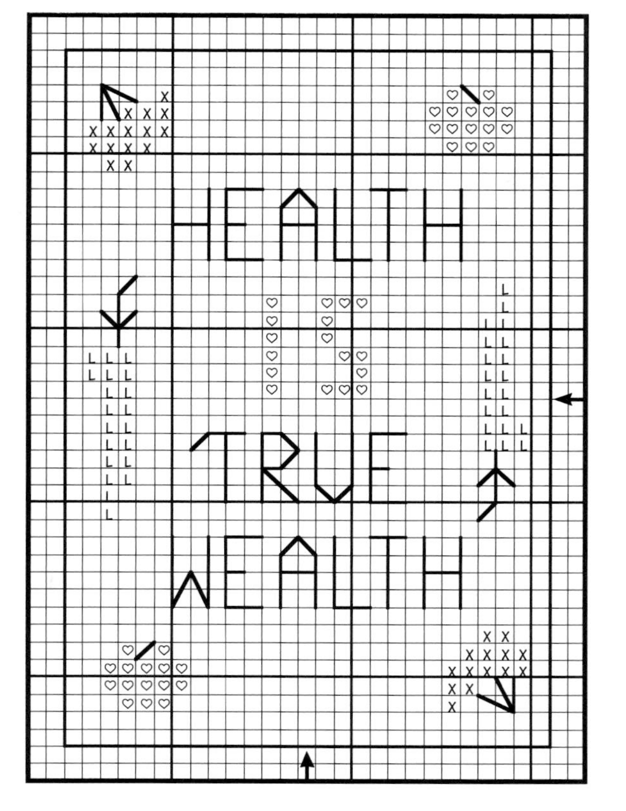

HEALTH IS TRUE WEALTH

	DMC	COLOR
X	909	emerald, vy. dk.
♡	321	red
L	721	spice, med.

Fabric: 14-count white Aida
Stitch count: 40H x 27W
Design size:
14-count 2⅞" x 2"

Instructions: Cross stitch using two strands of floss. Backstitch using two strands 909.

EAT SMART

	DMC	COLOR
y	725	topaz
♡	321	red
•	310	black

Fabric: 14-count white Aida
Stitch count: 40H x 27W
Design size:
14-count 2⅞" x 2"

Instructions: Cross stitch using two strands of floss. Backstitch using two strands 321.

EAT DESSERT FIRST

	DMC	COLOR
•	898	coffee brown, vy. dk.
R	321	red
V	745	yellow, lt. pl.
C	3772	flesh, dk.
S	963	dusty rose, vy. lt.
–	white	white
bs	799	delft, med.

Fabric: 27-count cream Linda cloth from Zweigart®
Stitch count: 27H x 31W
Design size:
26-count 2" x 2⅜"

Instructions: Cross stitch over two threads using two strands of floss. Backstitch using one strand of floss.
Backstitch (bs) instructions:
799 bowl
898 cherry stems, lettering

(Rectagular acrylic magnets from Lechter's Housewares; square acrylic magnet from Wheatland Crafts, Inc., 834 Scuffletown Road, Simpsonville, SC 29681, 1-800-334-7706.)

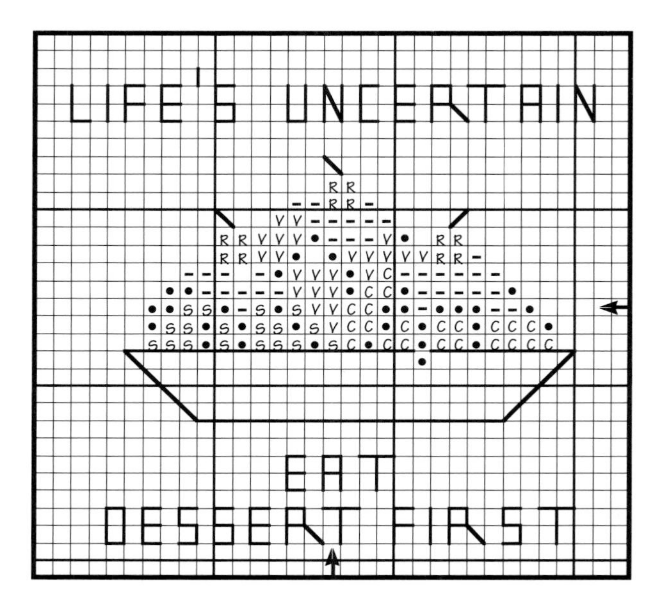

Southwestern Stitchery and Red Chilies

Emblems with a Southwestern influence have made their mark on the decorating scene. Create these designs on items for a pleasing desert-inspired theme in your kitchen. Stitch with bright floss colors on black place mats for a dramatic look. The designs take on a completely different appearance when worked in pastels. Charts are on page 80.

SOUTHWESTERN STITCHERY AND RED CHILIES

Bright Colors

	DMC	COLOR
O	946	burnt orange, med.
M	606	orange-red
•	321	red
▲	905	parrot green, dk.
X	907	parrot green, lt.
B	435	brown, vy. lt.
L	677	old gold, vy. lt.

Pastel Colors

	DMC	COLOR
L	ecru	ecru
B	778	mauve, lt.
X	564	jade, vy. lt.
M	3042	antique violet, lt.

Fabrics: ***Black Place Mats***—28-count linen used as waste canvas; ***Green Napkins***—20-count linen used as waste canvas

Stitch count:

Coyote	35H x 28W
Red Chilies	28H x 12W
Cactus	23H x 18W
Pastel Cactus	23H x 18W

Design size:

Coyote	28-count	2½" x 2"
	20-count	3½" x 2⅞"
Red Chilies	28-count	2" x ⅞"
Cactus	28-count	1⅝" x 1¼"
Pastel Cactus	20-count	2⅜" x 1⅞"

Black Place Mats (Photo is on page 79.)
Instructions: Cross stitch over two threads using two strands of floss. Backstitch chili pepper stems using two strands 905. Stitch *Cactus* 1½" down from upper fabric edge and 1" in from left fabric edge. Stitch *Coyote* 1½" up from lower fabric edge and 1" in from left fabric edge. Center *Red Chilies* between *Cactus* and *Coyote* and stitch 1" in from left fabric edge.

Green Napkins (Photo is on page 78.)
Instructions: Cross stitch over two threads using two strands of floss. Backstitch chili pepper stems using two strands 905. Stitch designs in lower-left corner 1" from fabric edges using pastel color code.

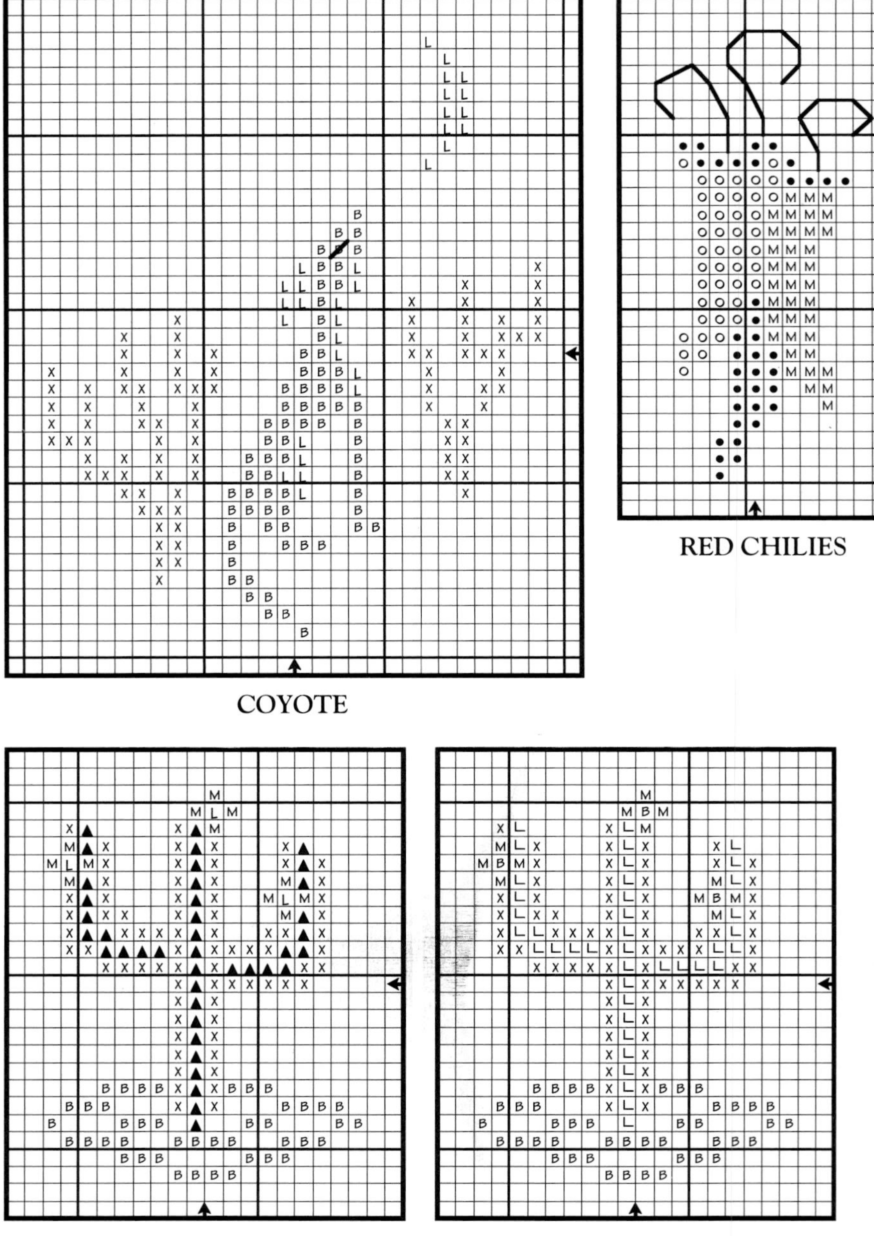

Calico Rooster

Every country kitchen needs a crowing rooster to start the day off right, and this eye-opening barnyard favorite will be a winner even with those who feel they're allergic to morning. This cheery fellow will be right at home on an apron, a bread cover, even a denim skirt.

	DMC	COLOR
•	930	antique blue, dk.
6	931	antique blue, med.
=	932	antique blue, lt.
✳	349	coral, dk.
V	783	gold
O	725	topaz
/	3341	apricot
3	471	avocado, vy. lt.

Fabric: 16-count antique ivory Aida from Wichelt Imports, Inc.
Stitch count: 17H x 16W
Design size:
16-count 2⅛" x 2"

Instructions: Cross stitch over two threads using four strands of floss.

(Napkin holder 8891 from Sunshine Station, Post Office Drawer 2388, Hickory, NC 28603.)

ONLY THAT DAY DAWNS
TO WHICH WE ARE AWAKE
HD THOREAU
WELCOME

For the Home

Whimsical or traditional, needlework conveys hospitality and a warm, heartfelt welcome. Stitched decorative accessories add pizzazz to your home; in this chapter, you'll find quick-to-complete, easy-to-finish pieces both to display and to share.

LAVENDER

Pillow Pair

Add your personal touch to living room or den furnishings with this pair of easy-to-finish pillows. Tossed casually on chairs or a sofa, these pieces make ideal display spots for your handiwork while brightening your home. The pineapple, a traditional symbol of hospitality, imparts a cheerful welcome when stitched trio-style along with a single monogram initial. The quick-to-complete thistle, shown worked over four threads, gives the illusion of a larger, more time-consuming project. Charts are on page 86. Finishing instructions for pillows are on pages 142 and 143.

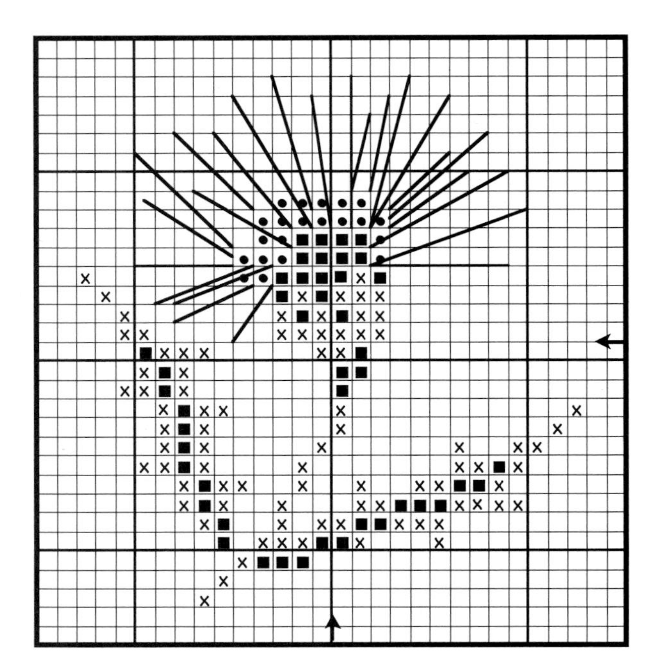

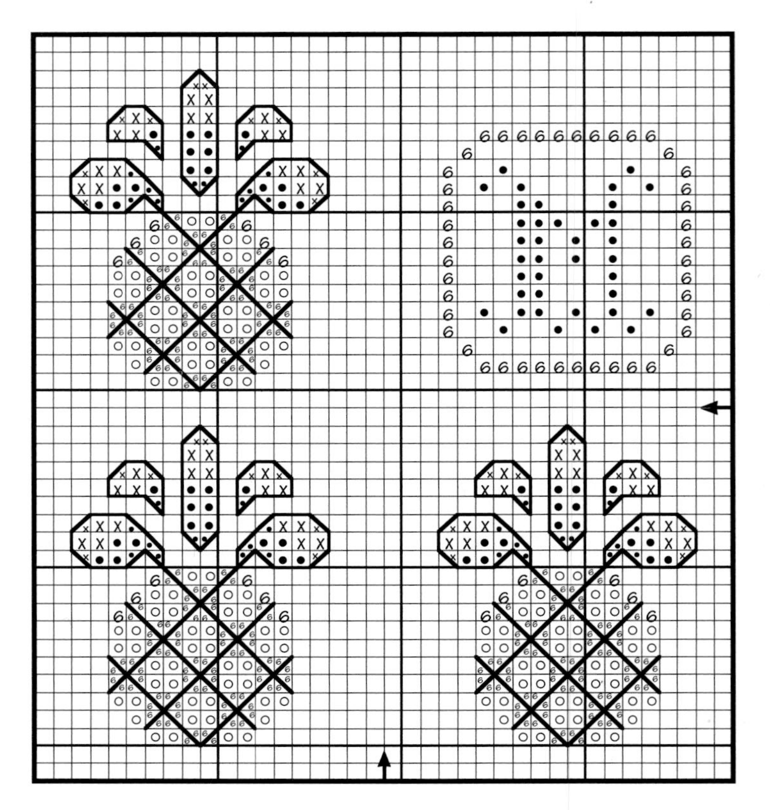

THISTLE

	DMC	COLOR
■	520	fern green, dk.
X	522	fern green
●	3328	salmon, med.
ss	760	salmon

Fabric: 18-count natural Glenora from Wichelt Imports, Inc.
Stitch count: 28H x 26W
Design size:
18-count 6¼" x 5¾"

Instructions: Cross stitch over four threads using six strands of floss. Separate strands of floss and put back together for stitching. Work straight stitches (ss) for flower using one strand each 760 and 3328. Finishing instructions are on page 142.

PINEAPPLE MONOGRAM

	DMC	COLOR
●	731	olive, dk.
X	733	olive, med.
6	781	topaz, dk.
○	783	gold

Fabrics: 14-count natural Dutch Garden from Wichelt Imports, Inc.
Stitch count:

Pillow	38H x 34W	
Initial	10H x 10W	

Design size:

Pillow	14-count	5½" x 4⅞"
Initial	14-count	1½" x 1½"

Instructions: Cross stitch over two threads using six strands of floss. Backstitch pineapples using three strands 731. Finishing instructions are on page 142.

(Chart for alphabet is on page 21.)

Miniature Houses

Featured on kitchen accessory pieces in chapter three, the *Miniature Houses* show their versatility stitched here along the edge of a plain pillowcase. Complete a matching pair of pillowcases with the houses worked in colors to match a couple's first home and present these bed linens to them as a lasting keepsake. Charts begin on page 62.

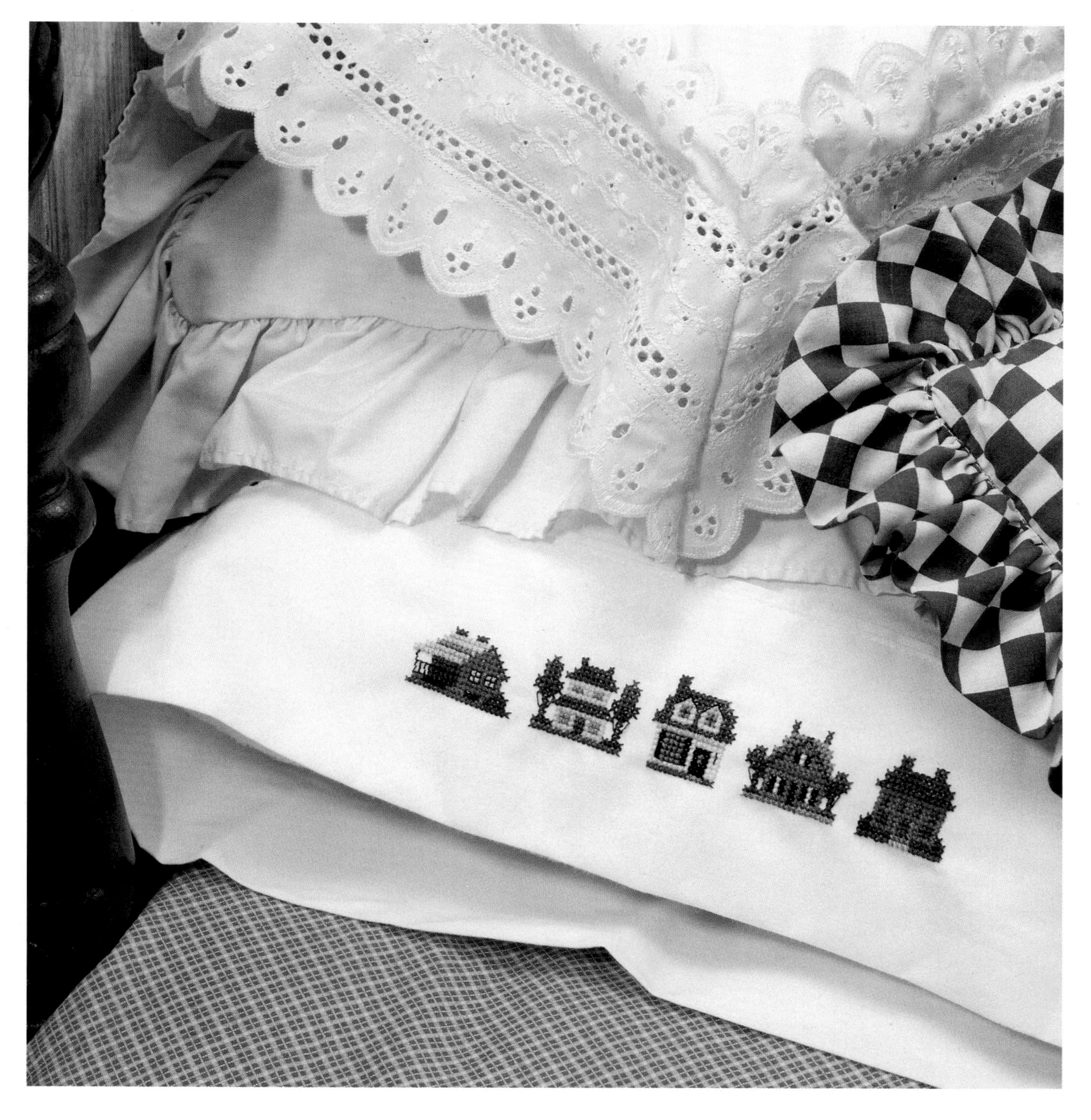

A "Welcome" Trio

Each of these charming designs conveys a message of friendliness to your visitors. Choose a single favorite or stitch all three for use in different areas. *Welcome* will fit splendidly on a peg rack in a country kitchen, and *Fruit Stack Welcome* will make a colorful accent for an entryway. *Back Door Welcome*, finished for hanging on a doorknob, sends a cheery hello to back door guests. Charts are on page 90. Finishing instructions are on page 142.

WELCOME
Jane -
Make yourself
at home. Will
be back soon.
Claudia
WELCOME

FRUIT STACK WELCOME

	DMC	COLOR
■	890	pistachio, ul. dk.
●	319	pistachio, vy. dk.
6	367	pistachio, dk.
/	725	topaz
=	741	tangerine, med.
V	349	coral, dk.
O	435	brown, vy. lt.
bs	730	olive, vy. dk.
bs	732	olive

Fabric: 20-count cream linen from Charles Craft, Inc.
Stitch count: 33H x 48W
Design size:
20-count 3⅜" x 4⅞"

Instructions: Cross stitch over two threads using four strands of floss. Backstitch using two strands of floss.
Backstitch (bs) instructions:
732 pineapple leaves
730 remainder of backstitching

(Bulletin board from Wheatland Crafts, Inc., 834 Scuffletown Road, Simpsonville, SC 29681, 1-800-334-7706.)

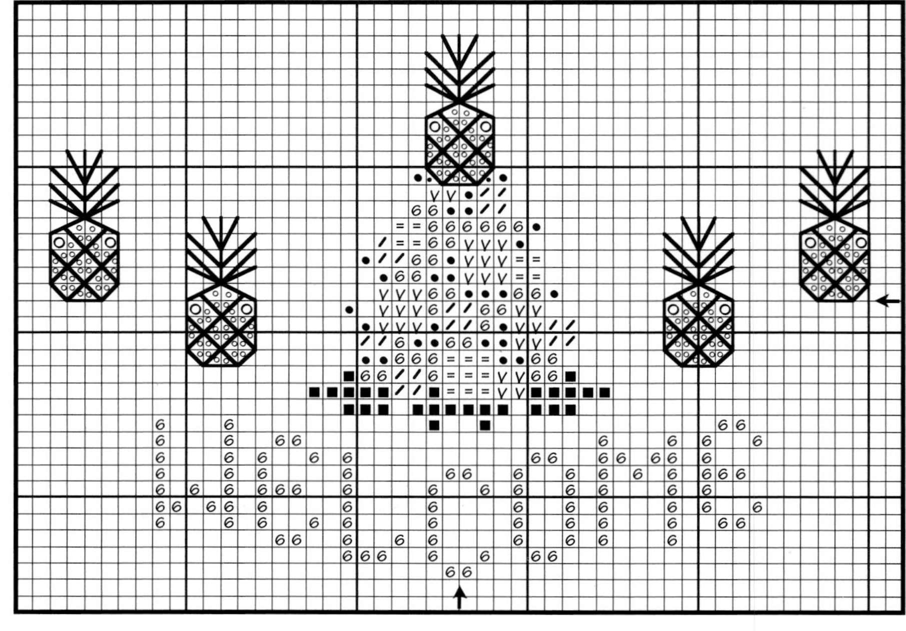
FRUIT STACK WELCOME

WELCOME

	DMC	COLOR
●	890	pistachio, ul. dk.
–	350	coral, med.
X	320	pistachio, med.

Fabric: 27-count cream Linda® Cloth from Zweigart®
Stitch count: 25H x 44W
Design size:
27-count 1⅞" x 3¼"

Instructions: Cross stitch over two threads using two strands of floss. Finishing instructions are on page 142.

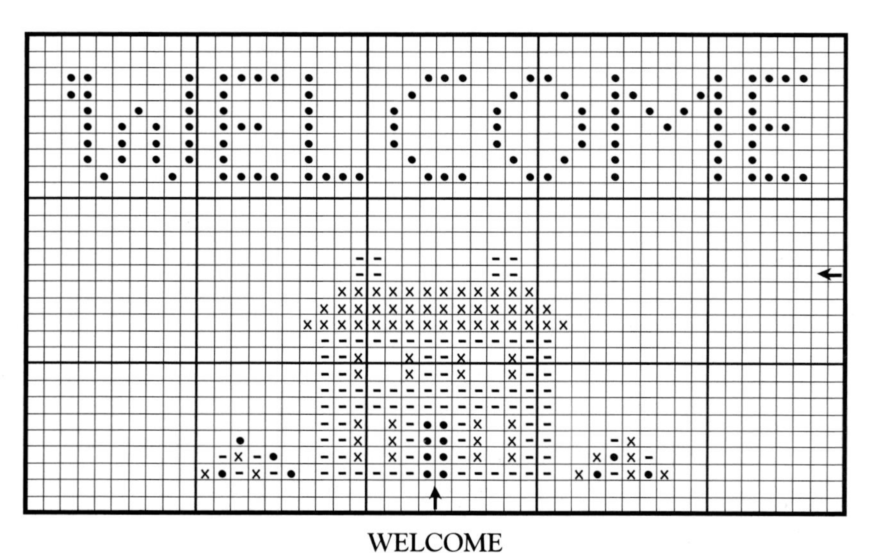
WELCOME

BACK DOOR WELCOME

	DMC	COLOR
■	349	coral, dk.
O	351	coral
●	825	blue, dk.
3	906	parrot green, med.
/	725	topaz
X	433	brown, med.
bs	310	black

Fabric: 20-count cream linen from Charles Craft, Inc.
Stitch count: 12H x 45W
Design size:
20-count 1¼" x 4½"

Instructions: Cross stitch over two threa using four strand of floss. Backstitch usi two strands of floss.
Backstitch (bs) instructions:
349 small hearts
310 remainder of backstitching

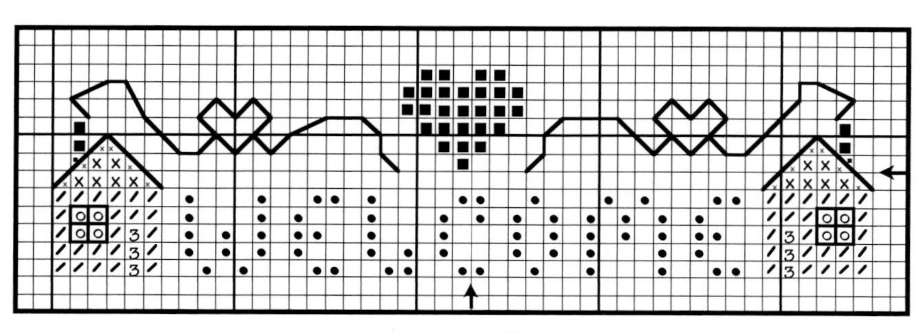
BACK DOOR WELCOME

Finishing instructions are on page 142.

Notable Quote

When you have a tiny nook that needs a small accessory to make it complete, put needle and floss to fabric and stitch these words of wisdom from Henry David Thoreau. Change the ground fabric to suit your needs and place your finished work on a tabletop easel.

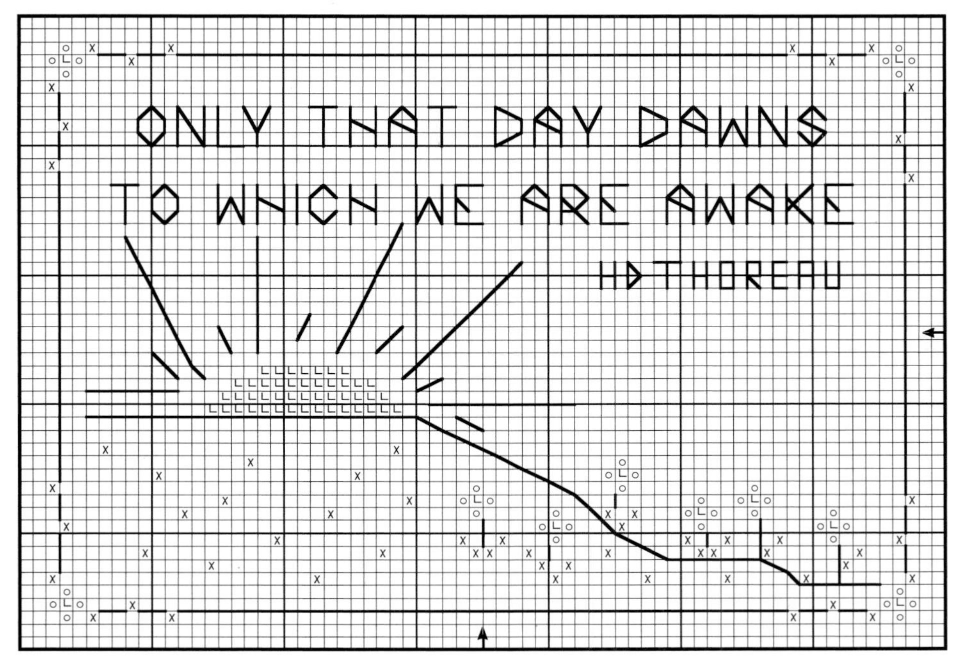

	DMC	COLOR
X	368	pistachio, lt.
L	727	topaz, vy. lt.
O	351	coral

Fabric: 14-count peach Aida from Charles Craft, Inc.
Stitch count: 45H x 66W
Design size:
14-count 3¼" x 4¾"

Instructions: Cross stitch using three strands of floss. Backstitch using two strands of floss.
Backstitch instructions:
351 lettering
727 sun's rays
368 remainder of backstitching

Home Sweet Home

Simple stitchery takes on fabulous appeal when it's designed to fit in purchased display pieces that make for quick, hassle-free finishing. A pair of feathered friends faces a large heart to complete this design, titled *Home Sweet Home*, which fills the window of an eye-catching birdhouse frame. The three-dimensional frame is a perfect complement for this cross-stitch piece. When used together, the frame and your completed needlework will add a hint of country charm in any home.

	DMC	COLOR
✳	517	Wedgwood, med.
V	518	Wedgwood, lt.
C	519	sky blue
▲	347	salmon, dk.
●	3328	salmon, med.
=	760	salmon
○	783	gold
/	ecru	ecru
bs	3371	black-brown

Fabric: 20-count cream linen from Charles Craft, Inc.
Stitch count: 37H x 30W
Design size:
20-count 3¾" x 3"

Instructions: Cross stitch over two threads using four strands of floss. Backstitch (bs) birds using two strands 3371. Make French knots for birds' eyes where ● appears at intersecting grid lines using three strands 3371, wrapping floss around needle once.

(Bird house frame from Wheatland Crafts, Inc., 834 Scuffletown Road, Simpsonville, SC 29681, 1-800-334-7706.)

Towel Twosome

Quick-stitch motifs, worked across the bands of cross-stitch towels for the bathroom, change small, fingertip driers into functional accessories with impact. The *Southwestern Motif* design features colors and figures with the south-of-the-border appeal that has become so fashionable in interior decorating, and the *Sampler Motif* design blends with this look. Together, these pieces will make splendid accents for the bathroom.

SOUTHWESTERN MOTIF

	DMC	COLOR
X	320	pistachio, med.
•	959	sea green, med.
W	356	terra cotta, med.
C	316	mauve, med.
/	676	old gold, lt.

Fabric: 14-count yellow Park Avenue Fingertips™ towel from Charles Craft, Inc.
Stitch count: 18H x 18W
Design size:
14-count 1¼" x 1¼"

Instructions: Cross stitch using two strands of floss. Stitch design three times, centering middle design on cross-stitch fabric panel and leaving six threads between each design.

SAMPLER MOTIF

	DMC	COLOR
•	3777	terra cotta, vy. dk.
W	355	terra cotta, dk.
+	356	terra cotta, med.
▲	3051	green-gray, dk.
/	677	old gold, vy. lt.
O	597	turquoise

Fabric: 14-count tan Park Avenue Fingertips™ towel from Charles Craft, Inc.
Stitch count: 21H x 18W
Design size:
14-count 1½" x 1¼"

Instructions: Cross stitch using two strands of floss. Stitch design three times, centering middle design on cross-stitch fabric panel and leaving ten threads between each design.

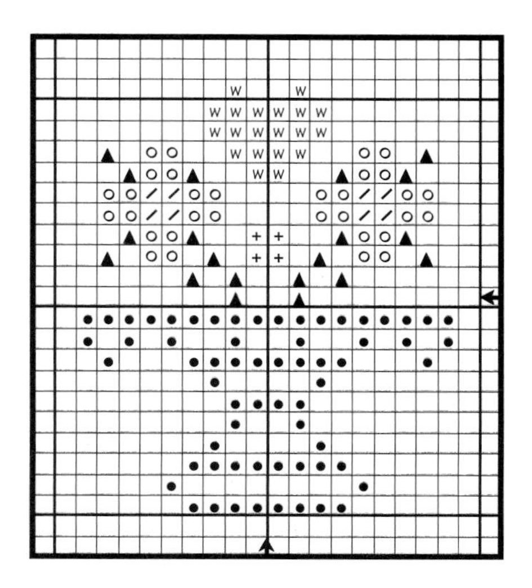

THANK
YOU
A SMILE
FOR YOU

For Gift Giving

A gift of stitchery is a treasure to the person who receives it, and it delivers a message that you cared enough to make a special memento for someone whose friendship you cherish. Choose from an assortment of prefinished pieces—from scissors cases to makeup bags—and work stitching magic on them for presents that make gift giving easy.

Hearts and Flowers

Teenage girls like to fill their bedrooms with pretty things, and your young miss will be pleasantly surprised with your gift of *Hearts and Flowers* stitchery worked on a lace-edged cone for her room! The same design, stitched on a pink sweatshirt, will be perfect for those all-night, all-fun, all-girl parties or for wearing with jeans for a casual look.

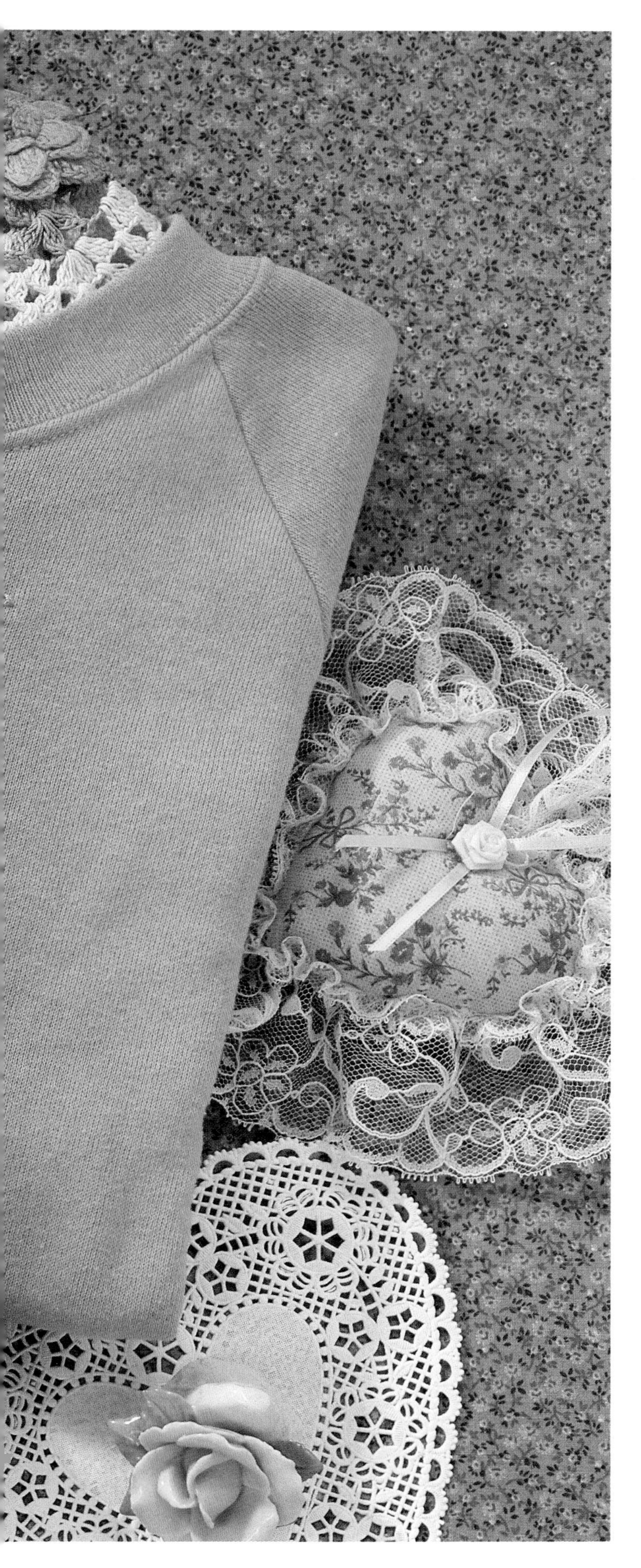

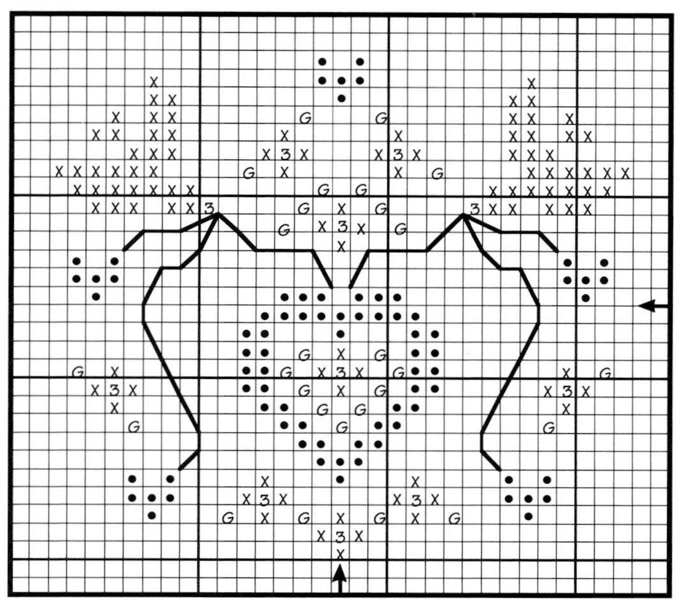

	DMC	COLOR
•	961	dusty rose, dk.
X	932	antique blue, lt.
3	744	yellow, pl.
G	320	pistachio, med.

Fabrics: ***Victorian Cone***—14-count pink Keepsake Cone from The JanLynn® Corporation; ***Sweatshirt***—20-count linen used as waste canvas on pink sweatshirt
Stitch count: 28H x 31W
Design size:
14-count 2" x 2¼"
20-count 2⅞" x 3⅛"

Victorian Cone
Instructions: Cross stitch using three strands of floss. Backstitch using two strands 961. Center design eight squares below top fabric edge.

Sweatshirt
Instructions: Cross stitch over two threads using four strands of floss. Backstitch using three strands 961. Center design 1" below neckline.

Special Occasions

A plant is a much-appreciated gift, particularly when it includes a stitched greeting instead of the usual handwritten card. Cross-stitched messages for use with plant spikes are terrific make-ahead projects. Complete several to have on hand when the need arises. Purchase the plastic card holders at a floral shop or craft store, and you can change an inexpensive potted plant into a lovely gift. This idea works well in a food basket sent to a new neighbor to town. Be sure to wash and dry the plastic holder before using, and then insert the sharp end into a loaf of homemade bread.

SPECIAL OCCASIONS PLANT SPIKES—GET WELL, FOR YOUR NEW HOME, A SMILE FOR YOU

	DMC	COLOR
⁘	676	old gold, lt.
V	725	topaz
\	444	lemon, dk.
X	347	salmon, dk.
C	3328	salmon, med.
II	760	salmon
♡	469	avocado
e	931	antique blue, med.
=	932	antique blue, lt.
W	433	brown, med.
■	310	black
–	white	white

Fabric: 14-count white Aida

Stitch count:

A Smile for You, For Your New Home	16H x 22W
Get Well	16H x 20W

Design size:

14-count

A Smile for You, For Your New Home	1⅛" x 1⅝"
Get Well	1⅛" x 1⅜"

Instructions: Cross stitch using two strands of floss. Backstitch using one strand of floss unless otherwise indicated. Backstitch all lettering using two strands of floss. Make French knots where ● appears at intersecting grid lines using two strands 310, wrapping

floss around needle once. Finishing instructions are on page 143.

Backstitch instructions:

310	all backstitching in *For Your New Home,* all backstitching **except** hearts in *A Smile For You*
469	stems in *Get Well*
347	hearts in *A Smile For You, Get Well*
931	flowers in *Get Well*

SPECIAL OCCASIONS PLANT SPIKES—THANK YOU, HAPPY 4TH, HAPPY BIRTHDAY

	DMC	COLOR
•	796	royal blue, dk.
▲	310	black
L	727	topaz, vy. lt.
G	320	pistachio, med.
B	3750	antique blue, vy. dk.
bs	321	red
bs	Metallic Thread	gold

Fabrics: ***Happy Birthday*** **and** ***Happy 4th***—14-count white Aida; ***Thank You***—14-count Blueridge Aida from Charles Craft, Inc.

Stitch count:

Thank You	27H x 34W
Happy 4th	20H x 42W
Happy Birthday	34H x 32W

Design size:

Thank You	14-count	2" x 2½"
Happy 4th	14-count	1½" x 3"
Happy Birthday	14-count	2½" x 2¼"

Instructions: Cross stitch using two strands of floss. Backstitch using two strands of floss. Finishing instructions are on page 143.

Backstitch (bs) instructions:

Thank You

3750	*Thank you,* flower petals
320	stems

Happy 4th

796	*th*
321	*4*
Metallic Thread	*Happy,* fireworks

Happy Birthday

321	confetti, *to you*
310	stems on musical notes
796	*Happy Birthday*

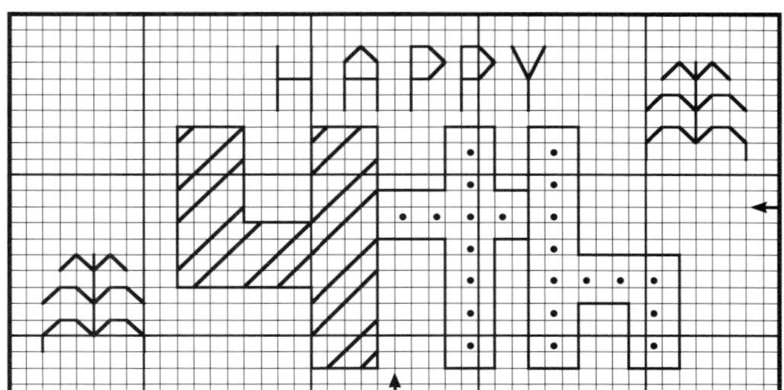

HAPPY 4TH

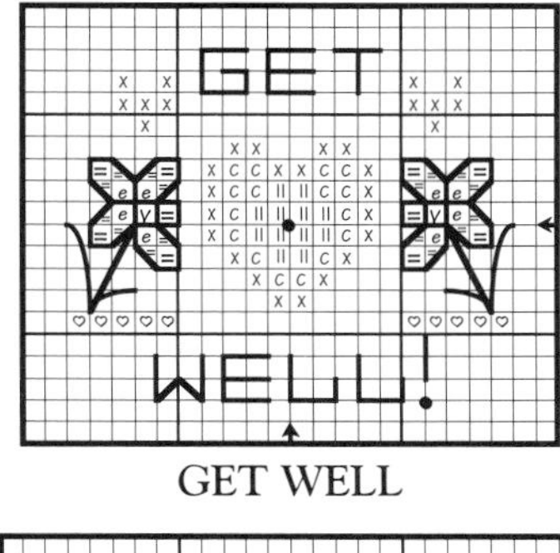

GET WELL

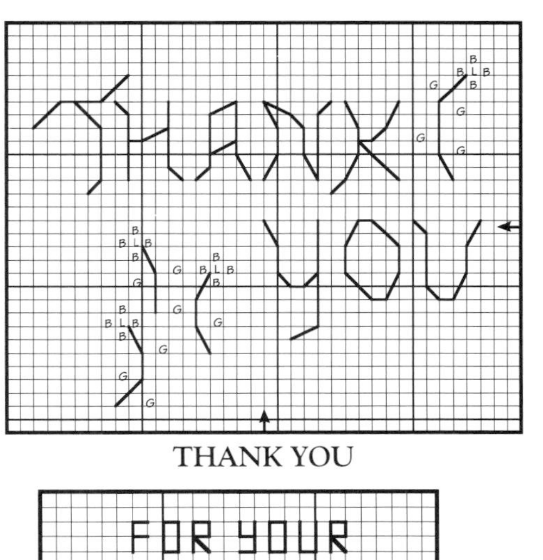

THANK YOU

HAPPY BIRTHDAY

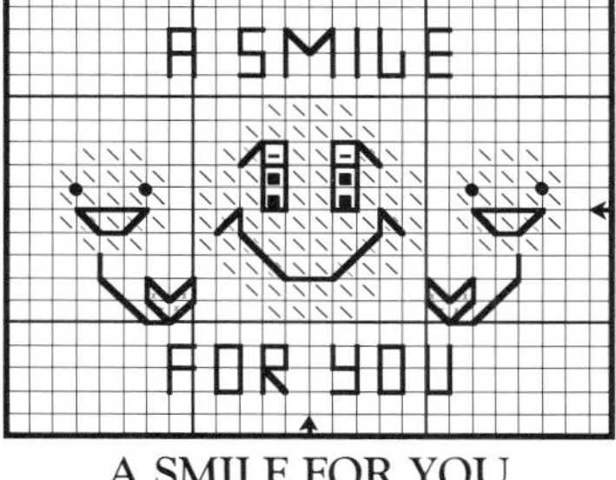

A SMILE FOR YOU

FOR YOUR NEW HOME

Tokens to Treasure

Small tokens of affection make thoughtful gifts, and young ladies will be especially pleased to receive them. If your little miss has a penchant for dazzling hair accessories, these colorful purchased hair bows trimmed with sparkling stitched butterflies will be definite winners. The trinket boxes, sporting a single butterfly and a trio of flower designs, will make precious hiding spots for tiny keepsakes. Choose a favorite or stitch an entire collection for that darling of yours. Get set for smiles and a warm hug when you give them to her.

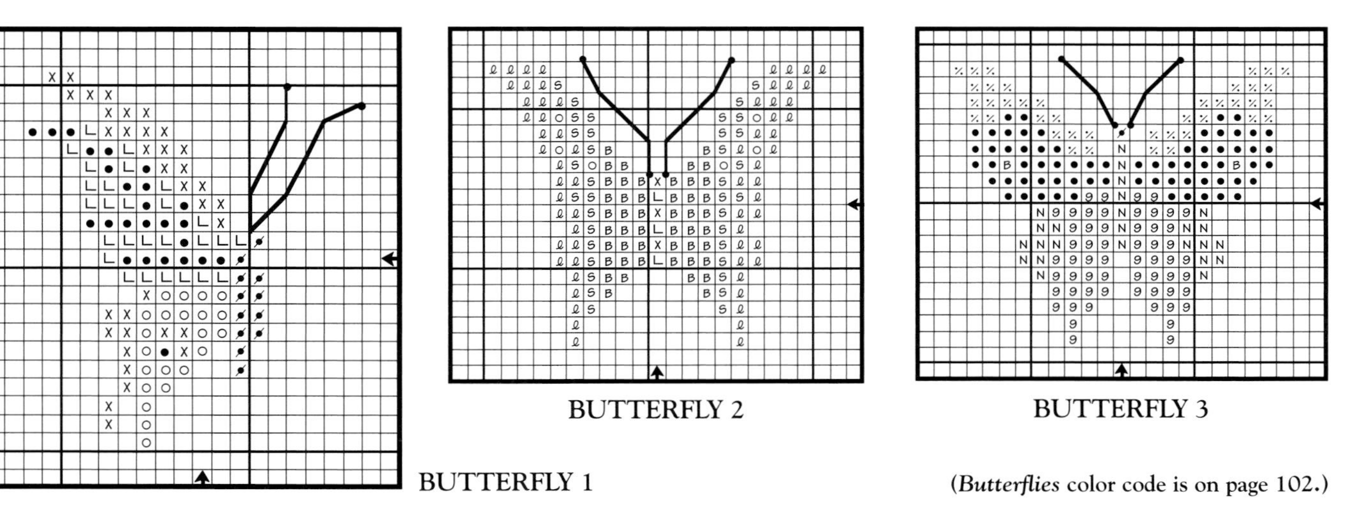

BUTTERFLY 1

BUTTERFLY 2

BUTTERFLY 3

(*Butterflies* color code is on page 102.)

BUTTERFLIES

	DMC	Kreinik Metallics	COLOR
⁄	310		black
o[	743		yellow, med.
		095BF	starburst
B[	333		blue-violet, dk.
		095BF	starburst
L[	741		tangerine, med.
		095BF	starburst
⁒[	699		green
		095BF	starburst
9[	815		garnet, med.
		095BF	starburst
X[	3341		apricot
		095BF	starburst
ℓ[	340		blue-violet, med.
		095BF	starburst
S[	208		lavender, vy. dk.
		095BF	starburst
•[	310		black
		005BF-HL	black
N[	797		royal blue
		095BF	starburst

Fabric: 18-count ivory Aida
Stitch count:
Butterfly 1 21H x 18W
Butterfly 2, Butterfly 3 18W x 21H
Design size:
18-count
Butterfly 1 1¼" x 1"
Butterfly 2, Butterfly 3 1" x 1¼"

Instructions: Cross stitch using two strands of floss. Backstitch antennae using one strand 310. Make French knots on ends of antennae using two strands 310, wrapping floss around needle once. When DMC and Kreinik Metallics are bracketed together, use one strand DMC and two strands Kreinik Blending Filament. Hair bow finishing instructions are on page 142.

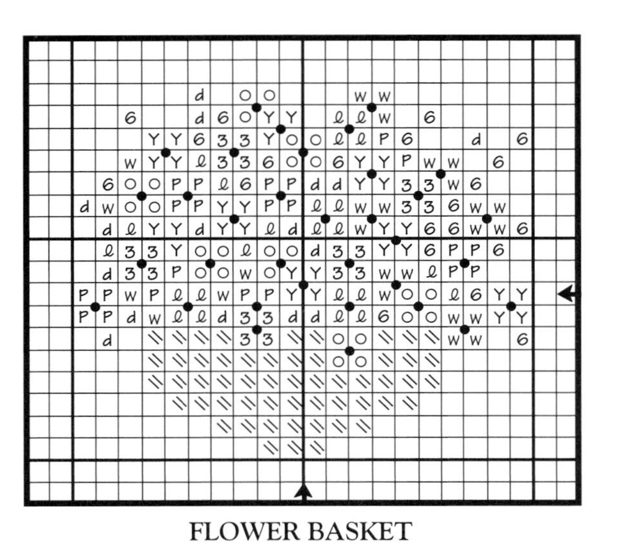

FLOWER BASKET

(Porcelain trinket boxes from Anne Brinkley Designs, 761 Palmer Avenue, Holmdel, NJ 07733.)

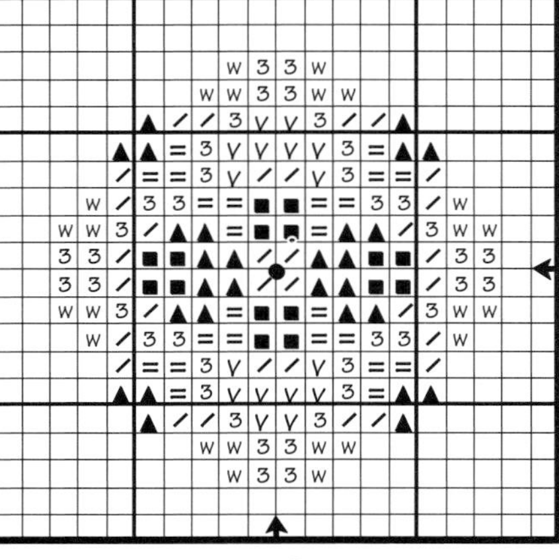

MAUVE FLOWER

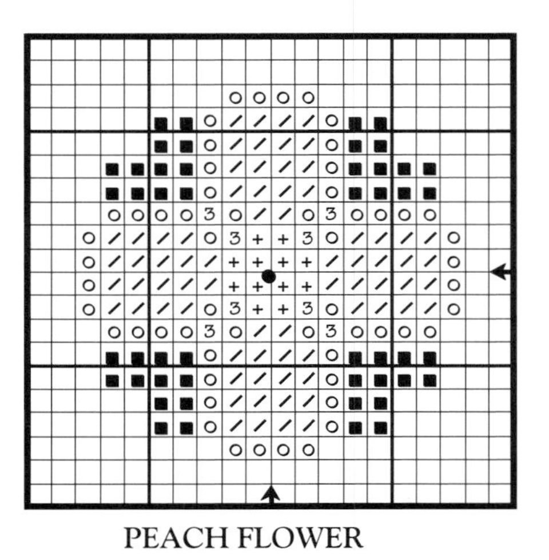

PEACH FLOWER

FLOWER BASKET

	DMC	COLOR
P	553	violet, med.
Y	743	yellow, med.
⑊	966	baby green, med.
3	783	gold
ℓ	799	delft, med.
O	321	red
W	550	violet, vy. dk.
6	522	fern green
d	520	fern green, dk.
Fk	922	copper, lt.

Fabric: 18-count ivory Aida
Stitch count: 17H x 20W
Design size:
18-count 1" x 1⅛"

Instructions: Cross stitch using two strands of floss. Make French knots (Fk) where • appears at intersecting grid lines using three strands 922, wrapping floss around needle once.

MAUVE FLOWER

	DMC	COLOR
■	930	antique blue, dk.
V	931	antique blue, med.
▲	902	garnet, vy. dk.
=	316	mauve, med.
3	319	pistachio, vy. dk.
⁄	676	old gold, lt.
W	315	mauve, dk.

Fabric: 27-count off-white linen from Norden Crafts
Stitch count: 16H x 16W
Design size:
27-count 2⅜" x 2⅜"

Instructions: Cross stitch over four threads using six strands of floss. Make French knot where • appears at intersecting grid lines in center of flower using three strands 315, wrapping floss around needle once.

PEACH FLOWER

	DMC	COLOR
■	350	coral, med.
⁄	white	white
O	353	peach flesh
+	725	topaz
3	469	avocado

Fabric: 25-count peach Lugana® from Zweigart®
Stitch count: 16H x 16W
Design size:
25-count 1⅜" x 1⅜"

Instructions: Cross stitch over two threads using two strands of floss. Make French knot where • appears at intersecting grid lines in center of flower using three strands 469, wrapping floss around needle once.

Teatime

Tea parties are an important part of a little girl's playtime. For many, the joy they held for us as youngsters carries over into our adult lives. If you recall fondly the tea parties of your childhood each time you sip a cup of tea, you'll love this endearing design, titled *Teatime*, that makes a plain canning jar an ideal container for holding your spiced tea. For an afternoon to remember, invite your daughter or granddaughter to join you. Present her with a home-baked, cellophane-wrapped cookie slipped inside a miniature tote bag with the *Tea Party* cross-stitch design, and celebrate the afternoon's festivities together. Chart for *Tea Party* is on page 65.

	DMC	COLOR
•	601	cranberry, dk.
+	603	cranberry
/	604	cranberry, lt.
3	825	blue, dk.
O	725	topaz
X	911	emerald, med.
Z	400	mahogany, dk.

Fabric: 18-count white Tabby Cloth from Zweigart®
Stitch count: 18H x 20W
Design size:
18-count 2" x 2¼"

Instructions: Cross stitch over two squares using four strands of floss. Backstitch using two strands of floss.
Backstitch instructions:
601 lettering, hearts, tea cup, saucer
825 steam rising from cup
911 stems

(*Blue Sampler* dinnerware from *Just CrossStitch*®, 405 Riverhills Business Park, Birmingham, AL 35242, 1-800-768-5878.)

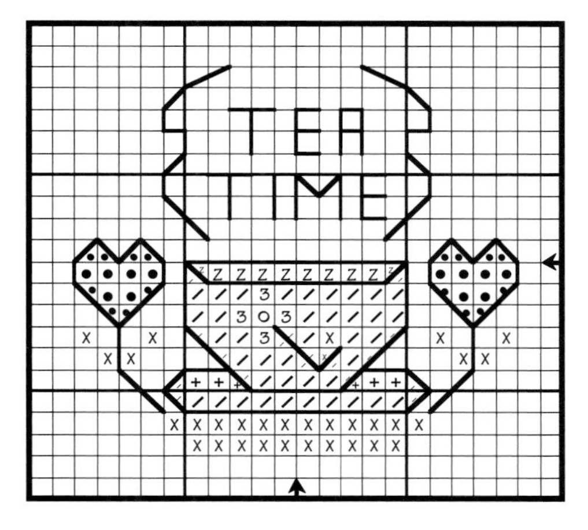

Totes Duo

Totes keep things organized, whether you're at home or on the go; and you can never have too many of them. If you are a needlework enthusiast who positively refuses to go anywhere without your stitching supplies, a large canvas carryall wearing the *Sewing Tools* design will allow you to show off your skills while keeping together all the materials you'll need to complete a project. Place your filled carrier in an out-of-the-way spot while at home and keep it close by in the car while on vacation or waiting for the kids to finish their soccer practice or piano lessons. If you collect footwear the way some women collect earrings and other accessories, a large tote will be an absolute necessity for you while traveling. Pack extra pairs of shoes in this durable bag stitched with assorted styles, and free up the space in your suitcase for other important items. Chart for *Shoes* is on page 106.

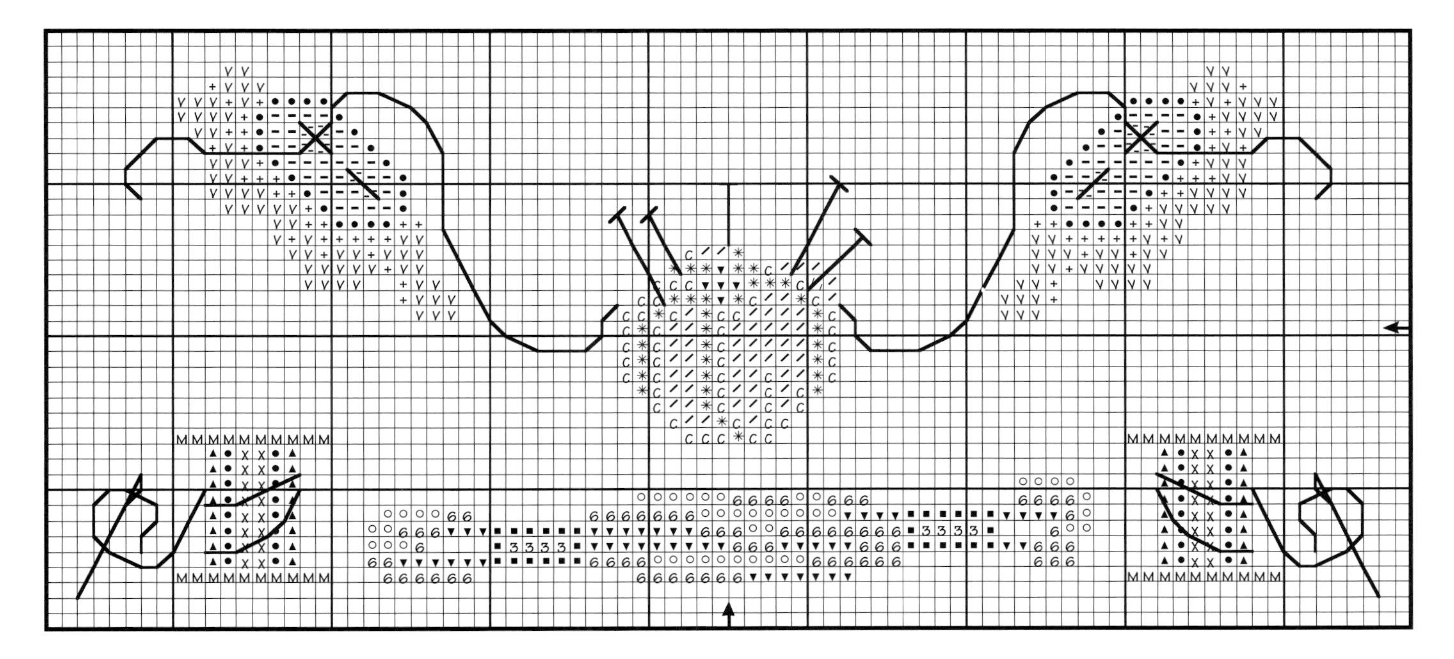

SEWING TOOLS

	DMC	COLOR
▲	517	Wedgwood, med.
•	518	Wedgwood, lt.
X	519	sky blue
■	310	black
3	680	old gold, dk.
M	434	brown, lt.
+	611	drab brown, dk.
V	612	drab brown, med.
–	613	drab brown, lt.
▼	319	pistachio, vy. dk.
6	367	pistachio, dk.
o	320	pistachio , med.
*	347	salmon, dk.
C	3328	salmon, med.
/	3712	salmon, med.
bs	413	pewter gray, dk.

Fabric: 6-count cross-stitch fabric panel on Canvas Big Bag from The JanLynn® Corporation

Stitch count: 35H x 82W

Design size:

6-count 5⅞" x 13⅝"

Instructions: Cross stitch using six strands of floss. Backstitch using three strands of floss. Center design on cross-stitch fabric panel of bag.

Backstitch (bs) instructions:

Backstitch in order listed.

413	straight pins, needles
3328	thread running from needles in fabric to pincushion
517	thread running from spools to needles

SHOES

	DMC	COLOR
R	321	red
I	825	blue, dk.
+	white	white
V	209	lavender, dk.
•	310	black
X	701	green, lt.
∩	839	beige-brown, dk.
O	444	lemon, dk.
T	958	sea green, dk.
♡	962	dusty rose, med.

Fabric: 20-count linen used as waste canvas on cream carryall tote
Stitch count: 53H x 91W
Design size:
20-count 5⅜" x 9"

Instructions: Cross stitch over two threads using four strands of floss. Backstitch using two strands of floss. Center design 2" below top edge of bag.
Backstitch instructions:
825 tennis shoe
839 green espadrille
962 puff on slipper
209 tassel on purple pump
958 "flip-flop"
310 remainder of backstitching

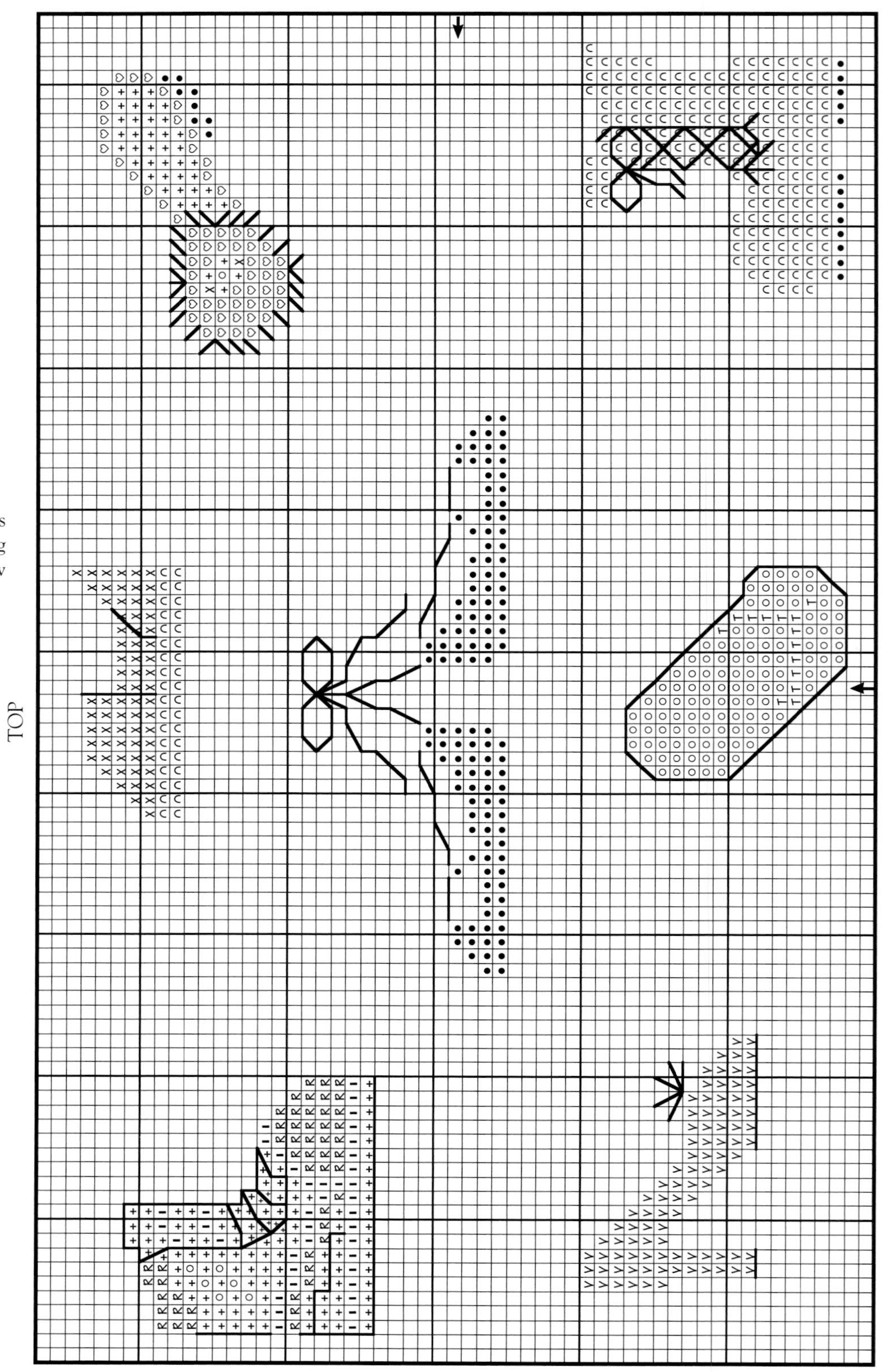

Make Me Beautiful

Every woman likes a nice storage spot for her cosmetics, and this purchased piece is the perfect size to fit into a purse or overnight case. It also makes a thoughful present for your daughter when she begins wearing makeup, and she will be thrilled that you consider her "grown-up!"

	DMC	COLOR
■	823	navy, dk.
∩	959	sea green, med.
/	744	yellow, pl.
L	340	blue-violet, med.
○	962	dusty rose, med.
•	519	sky blue

Fabric: 14-count ivory Aida panel on Newport Personal Pocket from The JanLynn® Corporation
Stitch count: 28H x 68W
Design size:
14-count 2" x 4⅞"

Instructions: Cross stitch using two strands of floss. Backstitch using two strands 823. Center design nine squares above lower edge of cross-stitch fabric panel.

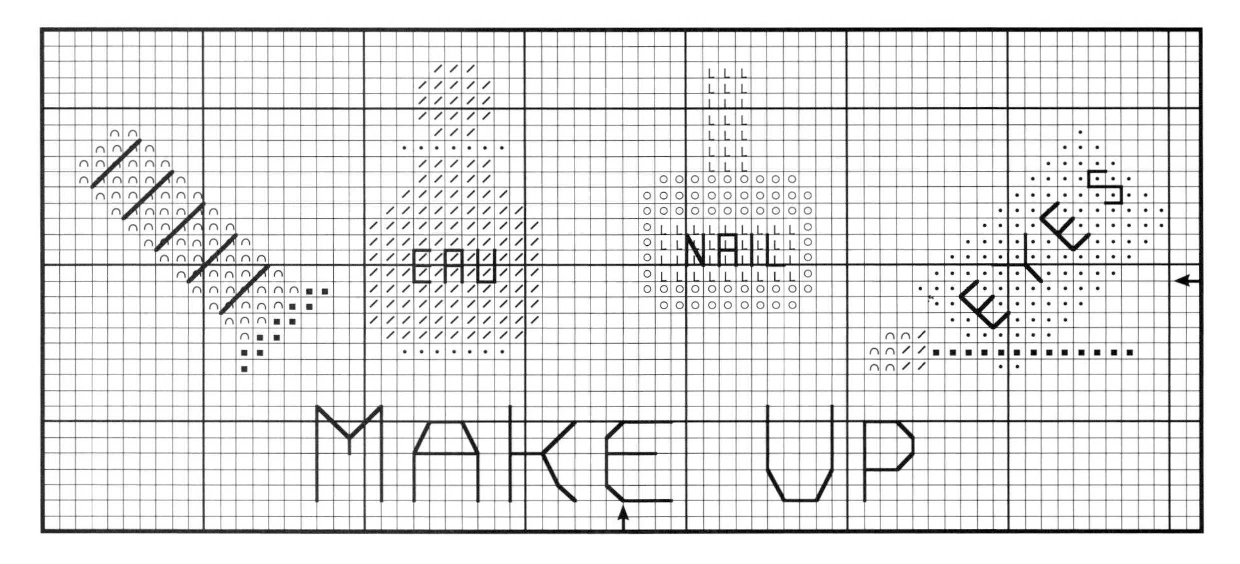

Bookmark Trio

Bookmarks are great for teachers; and this design titled *Apples for the Teacher* is sure to earn a smile from your child's educator. If your youngster has an interest in books and reading, encourage her with stitched page markers. The edged bands used for these bookmarks only require fringing to finish. You can have an assortment of pieces by varying the designs used. Charts for *Watermelons* and *School Days* are on page 14.

APPLES FOR THE TEACHER

	DMC	COLOR
•	white	white
a	349	salmon, dk.
G	561	jade, vy. dk.
Y	725	topaz
B	400	mahogany, dk.

Fabric: 18-count cream Aida Ribband® with forest green trim from Leisure Arts
Stitch count: 109H x 17W
Design size:
18-count 6⅛" x 1"

Instructions: Cross stitch using two strands of floss. Backstitch using one strand of floss.
Backstitch instructions:
400 stems
349 *APPLES* at top of design
561 remainder of lettering

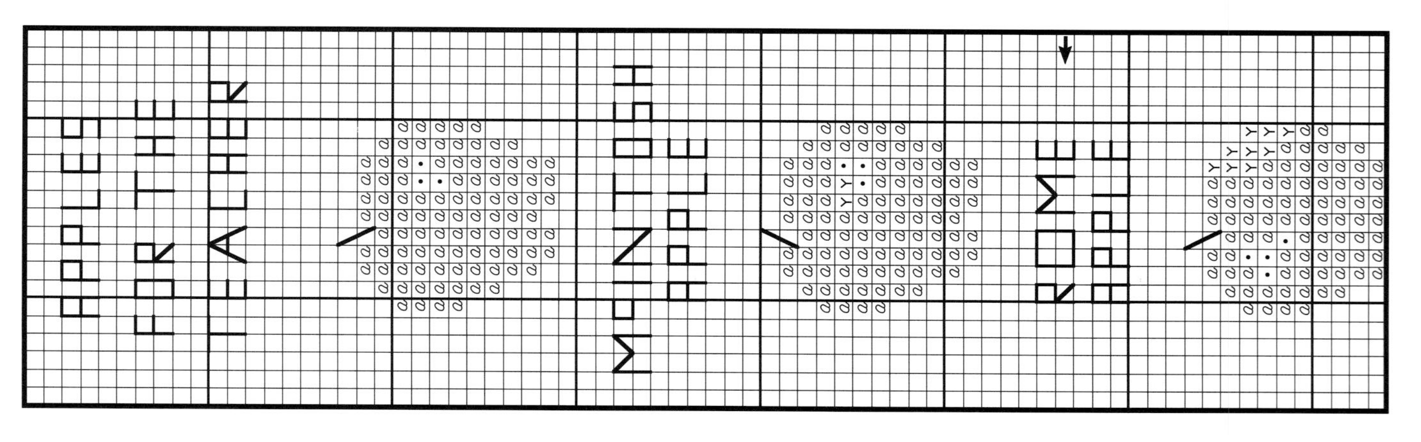

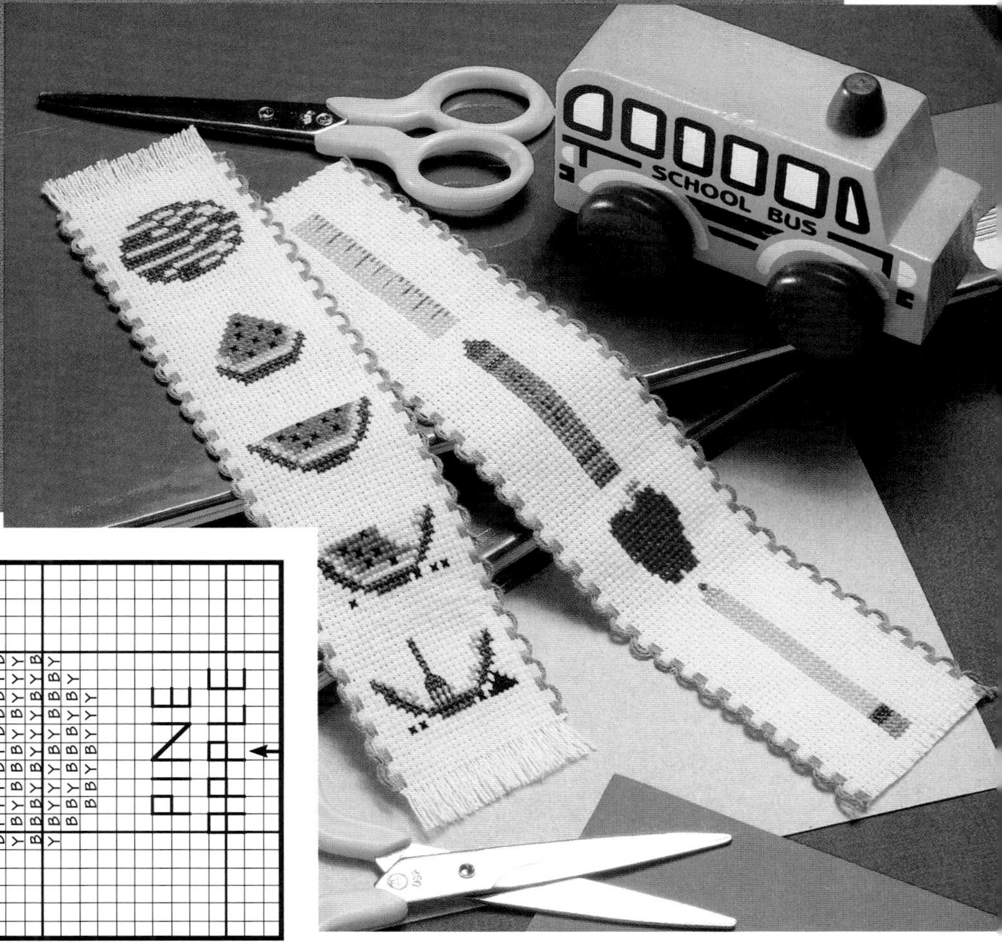

Shaded portion indicates overlap from previous page.

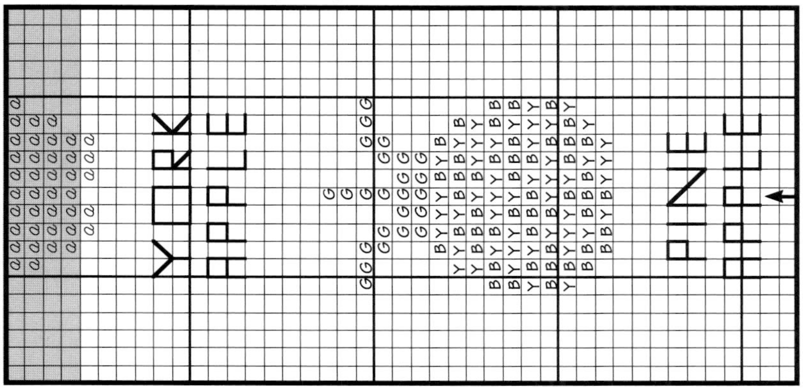

Ivy Wreath and Swag

Stitched ivy makes an unexpected appearance on winter warmers that are just the things to give or to keep. Backstitch and cross stitch are combined to form the delicate *Ivy Wreath* design trimming this matched set. A white cross-stitch fabric cone with the *Ivy Swag* design will make a splendid holder for trinkets of all types at Christmastime.

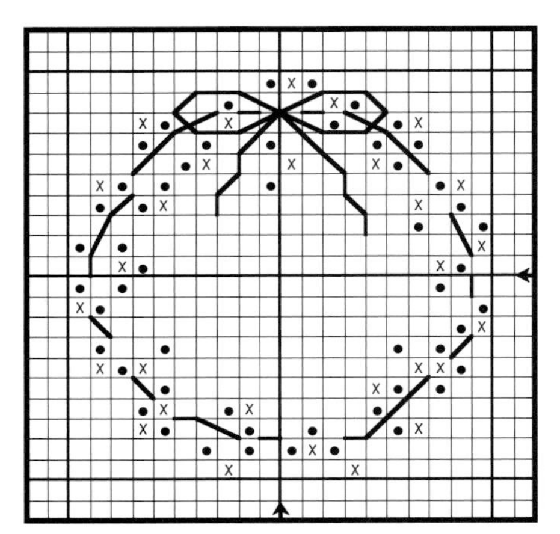

IVY WREATH

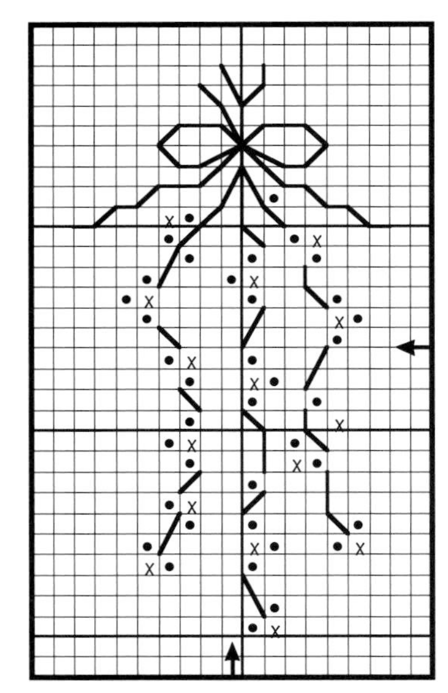

IVY SWAG

	DMC	COLOR
X	503	blue-green, med.
•	501	blue-green, dk.
bs	500	blue-green, vy. dk.
bs	304	red, med.

Fabrics: ***Scarf***—20-count linen used as waste canvas on white scarf; ***Hat***—28-count linen used as waste canvas on white hat; ***Cone***—14-count white Keepsake Cone from The JanLynn® Corporation

Stitch count:

Ivy Wreath	20H x 20W
Ivy Swag	28H x 15W

Design size:

Ivy Wreath	20-count	2" x 2"
	28-count	1½" x 1½"
Ivy Swag	14-count	2" x 1⅛"

Scarf and Hat

Instructions: Cross stitch over two threads using three strands of floss. Backstitch using two strands of floss. Center wreath on scarf 2" above lower edge. Center wreath on turned-up cuff of hat.

Cone

Instructions: Cross stitch using three strands of floss. Backstitch using two strands of floss. Center design 15 squares below top edge of cone.

Backstitch (bs) instructions:

500	ivy stems
304	bows

Vine Alphabet

Meandering vines and flowers form the letters of the intricate *Vine Alphabet*. The letters, ideal for monogramming, are featured in chapter one on the winter scarf on page 16 and are shown here worked on the band of a cross-stitch towel and on a tote. For a decidedly sophisticated look, stitch them on napkins, using linen in place of waste canvas, and present your efforts to a newly married couple. The tote, monogrammed with her new initials, will make a super shower gift for the bride. Chart begins on page 16.

Coral Flowers

Any stitcher would be glad to receive a set of personalized scissors cases for storing her prized cutting implements. Just the right size for tucking into a purse or small bag, these cloth cases, which come ready to stitch, can be taken along each time you embark on a trip. Spend your traveling time cross stitching, and you'll have a head start on finishing handmade pieces for birthdays and Christmas. Present your daughter a fine pair of scissors for her first sewing basket in one of these protective cases.

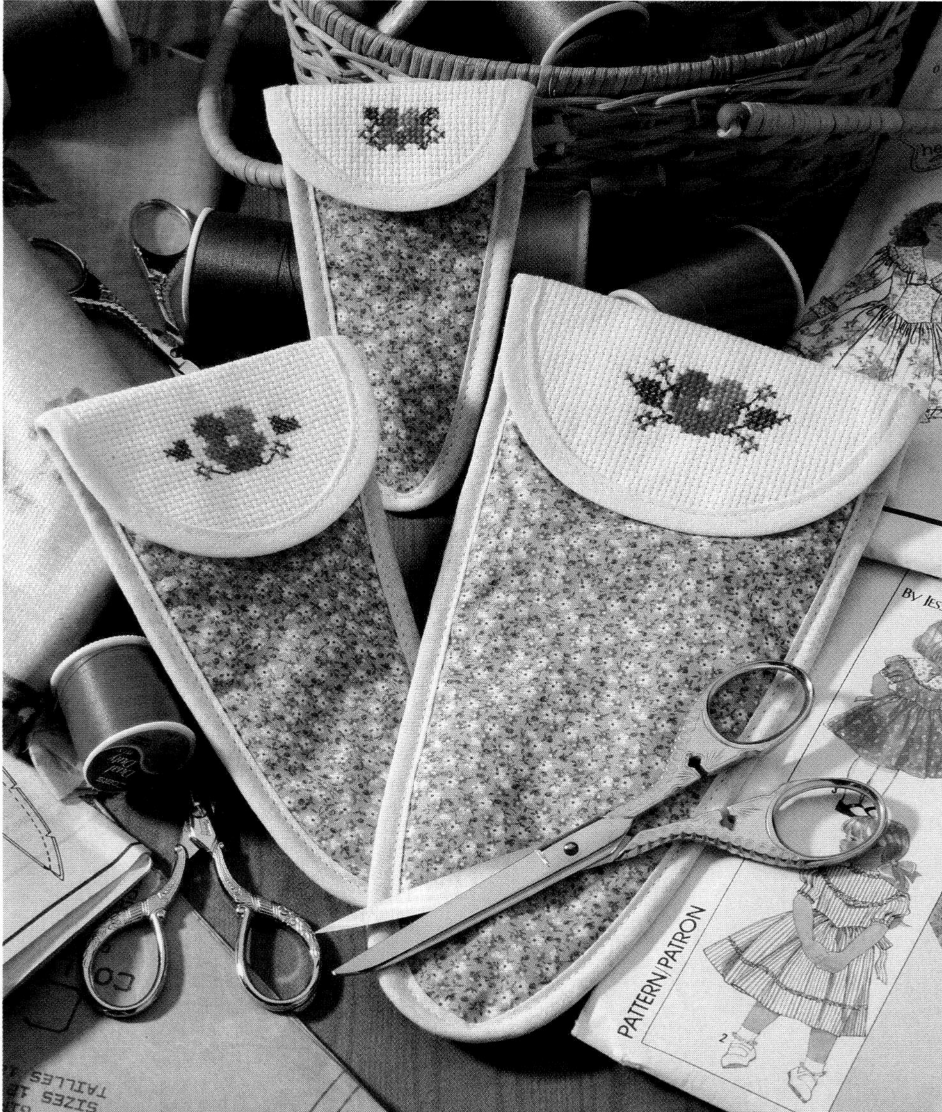

	DMC	COLOR
•	367	pistachio, dk.
3	350	coral, med.
X	351	coral
O	352	coral, lt.
/	ecru	ecru
V	931	antique blue, med.

Fabrics: 14-count cream Aida panel on Three Floral Scissors Cases from The JanLynn® Corporation

Stitch count:

Small	12H x 24W
Medium	10H x 20W
Large	7H x 13W

Design size:

Small	14-count	⅞" x 1¾"
Medium	14-count	¾" x 1½"
Large	14-count	½" x 1"

Instructions: Cross stitch using two strands of floss. Backstitch using one strand 367. Center design on cross-stitch fabric panel on flap of scissors cases.

LARGE

SMALL

MEDIUM

Fantastic Florals

Inspired by centuries-old all-white embroidery, this group of designs shows the versatility of cross stitch as well as the simple elegance it conveys when used on a variety of items. The *White Florals Quartet*, shown here, lends a refreshing new look to vintage table linens. *One-color Floral* features a single flower worked alone atop the flap of a scissors case. The same flower in another floss color, repeated across the band of a cross-stitch fingertip towel, shows how you can produce two entirely different looks using the same chart.

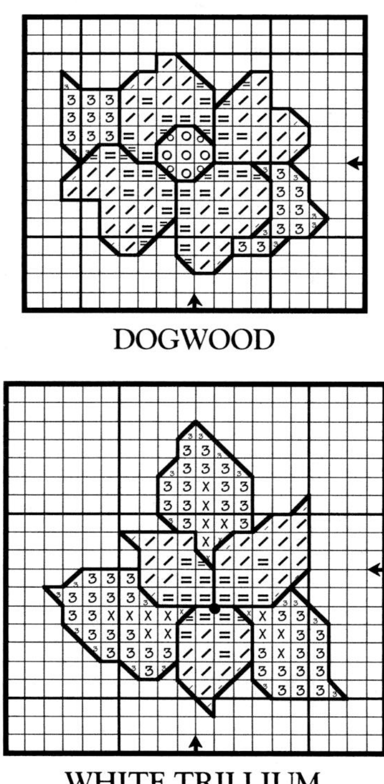

DOGWOOD

WHITE TRILLIUM

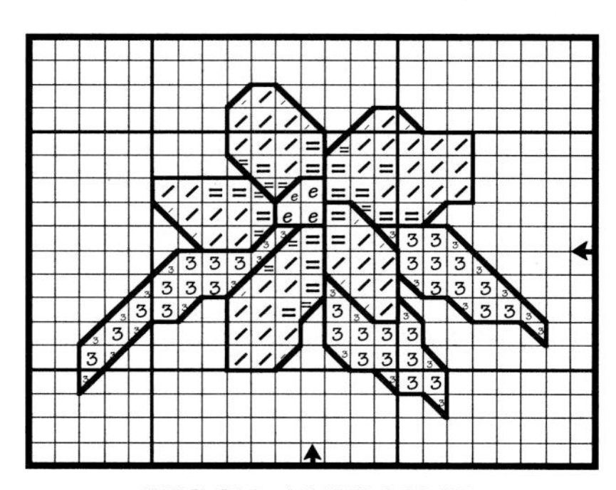

WOOD ANEMONE

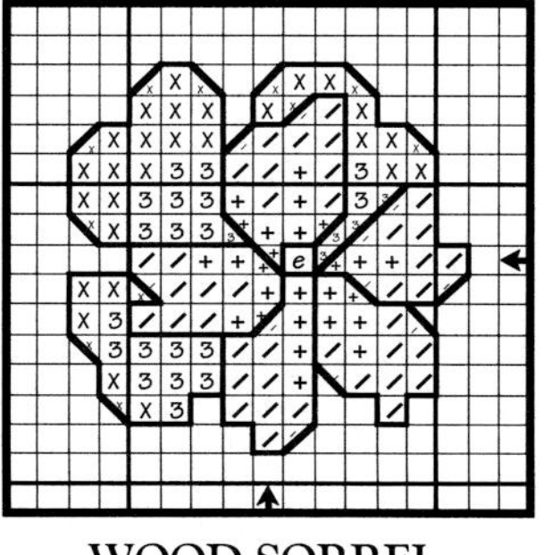

WOOD SORREL

WHITE FLORALS QUARTET

	DMC	COLOR
/	ecru	ecru
=	3033	mocha, vy. lt.
O	831	olive, med.
3	561	jade, vy. dk.
X	562	jade, med.
e	727	topaz, vy. lt.
+ [	ecru	ecru
	335	rose
bs	433	brown, med.
bs	3787	brown-gray, dk.

Fabric: 27-count linen used as waste canvas on green napkins

Stitch count:

Dogwood	12H x 14W
Wood Anemone	14H x 19W
White Trillium	16H x 16W
Wood Sorrel	13H x 13W

Design size:

Dogwood	27-count	⅞" x 1"
Wood Anemone	27-count	1" x 1⅜"
White Trillium	27-count	1¼" x 1¼"
Wood Sorrel	27-count	1" x 1"

Instructions: Cross stitch over two threads using two strands of floss. Backstitch using one strand of floss. After removing waste canvas, make a cluster of French knots in center of *White Trillium* using two strands 727, wrapping floss around needle once.
Backstitch (bs) instructions:

433	tips of dogwood petals
3787	flower petals, flower centers
561	leaves

ONE–COLOR FLORAL

	DMC	COLOR
X	ecru	ecru
	OR	
X	502	blue-green

Fabrics: ***Scissors Case***—14-count ecru Aida panel on Scissors Case from The JanLynn® Corporation; ***Towel***—14-count evergreen Aida panel on Park Avenue Fingertips™ towel from Charles Craft, Inc.
Stitch count: 17H x 25W
Design size:
14-count 1¼" x 1¾"

Scissors Case
Instructions: Cross stitch using three strands of floss. Backstitch using two strands of floss the same color as the cross stitches. Make French knots where • appears at intersecting grid lines using three strands of floss the same color as the cross stitches, wrapping floss around needle once. For scissors case, center design on cross-stitch fabric panel ten squares below top edge of panel.

Towel
Instructions: Cross stitch using three strands of floss. Backstitch using two strands of floss the same color as the cross stitches. Make French knots where • appears at intersecting grid lines using three strands of floss the same color as the cross stitches, wrapping floss around needle once. On towel, stitch design three times, centering middle design on cross-stitch fabric panel and leaving 14 squares between each design.

Pineapple Monogram

Complete a gift in record time using letters from the *Pineapple Monogram* alphabet. A purchased makeup bag and an umbrella can be personalized rapidly, making a clever and inexpensive present. The versatility of this design is evident in its varied uses. Chart begins on page 20.

Bluebirds and Hearts

A glasses case takes on marvelous appeal when it's trimmed with cross stitch. Combined with your handiwork, this ready-made case makes a no-finishing-needed project that is a snap to complete. Work the charming *Bluebirds and Hearts* design on a case to protect your eyeglasses, or present your finished piece to a bespectacled someone who shares your love for the art of the needle.

	DMC	COLOR
W	930	antique blue, dk.
=	367	pistachio, dk.
/	783	gold
o	760	salmon
X	3328	salmon, med.
▲	347	salmon, dk.
II	932	antique blue, lt.
Fk	3750	antique blue, vy. dk.

Fabric: 14-count cream Aida panel on Country Floral Eyeglass Case from The JanLynn® Corporation
Stitch count: 18H x 20W
Design size:
14-count 1¼" x 1½"

Instructions: Cross stitch using two strands of floss. Make French knots (Fk) for birds' eyes using one strand 3750, wrapping floss around needle once. Center design on cross-stitch fabric panel of eyeglass case.

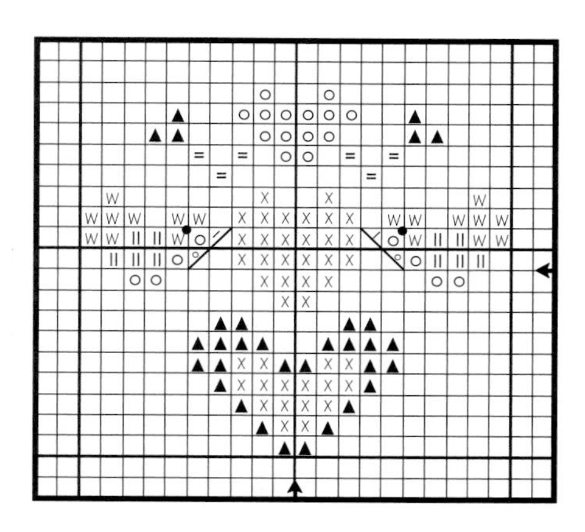

Ballet Slippers

These lovely pieces are certain to be favorites with your aspiring ballerina. The tote holds a small pair of ballet slippers, and the turtleneck is ideal for pulling on after a tough rehearsal. For extra appeal, add her name and the date of her first recital in freehand stitches to mark this important performance of her dancing career.

	DMC	COLOR
o	963	dusty rose, vy. lt.
bs	962	dusty rose, med.
bs	310	black

Fabrics: ***Tote***—14-count ivory Lil' Tote from The JanLynn® Corporation; ***Turtleneck***—28-count linen used as waste canvas on purple turtleneck
Stitch count: 31H x 17W
Design size:
14-count 2¼" x 1¼"
28-count 2¼" x 1¼"

Tote
Instructions: Cross stitch using three strands of floss. Backstitch using two strands of floss. Stitch design in upper-left corner nine squares below top edge and 13 squares in from side seam.

Turtleneck
Instructions: Cross stitch over two threads using three strands of floss. Backstitch using two strands of floss. Stitch design 1¼" in from sleeve seam and 2¼" below shoulder seam.

Backstitch (bs) instructions:
310 soles of slippers
962 remainder of backstitching

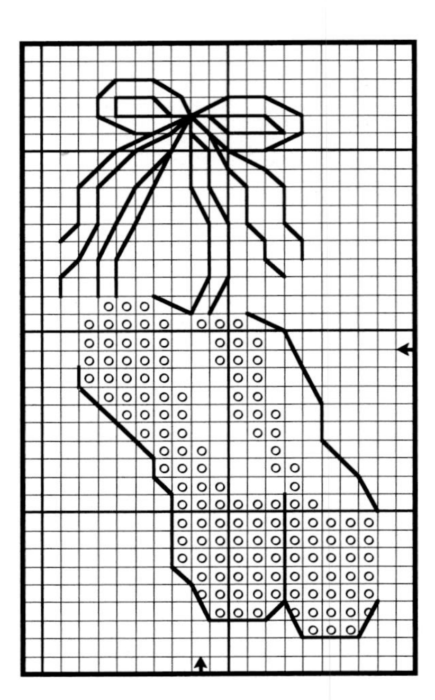

Welcome Baby

A new mom will appreciate a plant for the nursery or a tote filled with baby supplies. The "welcome-home-from-the-hospital" bag will keep baby's toys at Mom's fingertips. Finish the *Welcome Baby* design as a mini pillow for hanging on the nursery door.

	DMC	COLOR
/	727	topaz, vy. lt.
II	760	salmon
∪	564	jade, vy. lt.
=	932	antique blue, lt.
W	433	brown, med.
–	white	white
Fk	310	black
bs	562	jade, med.

Fabric: ***Plant Spike***—14-count white Aida; ***Tote***—14-count pink Aida Lil' Tote from The JanLynn® Corporation
Stitch count: 16H x 22W
Design size:
14-count
Plant Spike 1⅛" x 1⅝"
Tote 2⅜" x 3⅛"

Plant Spike

Instructions: Cross stitch using two strands of floss. Backstitch (bs) using two strands 562. Make French knots (Fk) where • appears at intersecting grid lines using two strands 310, wrapping floss around needle once. Finishing instructions are on page 143.

Tote

Instructions: Cross stitch over two squares using six strands of floss. Backstitch (bs) using three strands 562. Make French knots (Fk) where • appears at intersecting grid lines using three strands 310, wrapping floss around needle once. Center design on side of tote.

HAPPY
HOLIDAY
WITH
FOR MOM
JOY

For the Holidays

Smart needleworkers search throughout the year for holiday gift and decorating ideas. Included in this chapter are quick-stitch designs for special occasions from Valentine's Day to Halloween to Christmas. Put your nimble fingers to work to make these delightful keepsakes and enjoy the holidays in stitches.

Mini Ornaments

Trimming the Christmas tree is exciting, especially when you bring out your cherished handmade ornaments. Whether you already have a collection or you're just beginning one, you can make spectacular pieces for the evergreen in just a few hours. Be sure to date your creations in stitches within the designs or on the backs. Why not select one or two and make them for the one who taught you how to stitch? The inexpensive plastic snap-together frames make finishing a breeze and are commonly available at craft and needlework stores.

	DMC	COLOR
3	321	red
W	498	red, dk.
▲	890	pistachio, ul. dk.
6	367	pistachio, dk.
●	311	navy, med.
V	334	baby blue, med.
✳	783	gold
O	725	topaz
Z	433	brown, med.
╲	436	tan
L	738	tan, vy. lt.
■	310	black
=	415	pearl gray
/	white	white
⊙	754	peach flesh, lt.
I	948	peach flesh, vy. lt.
bs	413	pewter gray, dk.

Fabrics: 14-count white, emerald green, and navy Aida from Charles Craft, Inc.

(Color code continues on page 124.)

PEACE

Stitch count:

Rudolph	21H x 18W
Ho Ho Ho	21H x 22W
Tree	19H x 14W
Peace	20H x 26W
Angel	18H x 18W
Noel	18H x 18W
Snowman	19H x 14W
Angel Silhouette	18H x 17W
Package	16H x 14W
Santa	16H x 16W

Design size:

14-count

Rudolph	1½" x 1¼"
Ho Ho Ho	1½" x 1⅝"
Tree	1⅜" x 1"
Peace	1⅜" x 1⅞"
Angel	1¼" x 1¼"
Noel	1¼" x 1¼"
Snowman	1⅜" x 1"
Angel Silhouette	1¼" x 1¼"
Package	1⅛" x 1"
Santa	1⅛" x 1⅛"

Instructions: Cross stitch using two strands of floss. Backstitch using one strand of floss unless otherwise indicated. Make French knots using three strands of floss, wrapping floss around needle once.

Backstitch (bs) instructions:

367	tip of scarf in *Snowman*
311	all backstitching in *Angel*
310	all backstitching in *Rudolph*
413	all backstitching in *Santa*
890	*Merry Christmas* in *Ho Ho Ho*
321	ribbons on package beside tree, *Peace* in *Peace* (two strands)
725	star in *Tree*

French knot instructions:

310	snowman's smile
white	center of Rudolph's eyes
321	holly berries, center of bow on large package, tree ornaments, berries on wreath

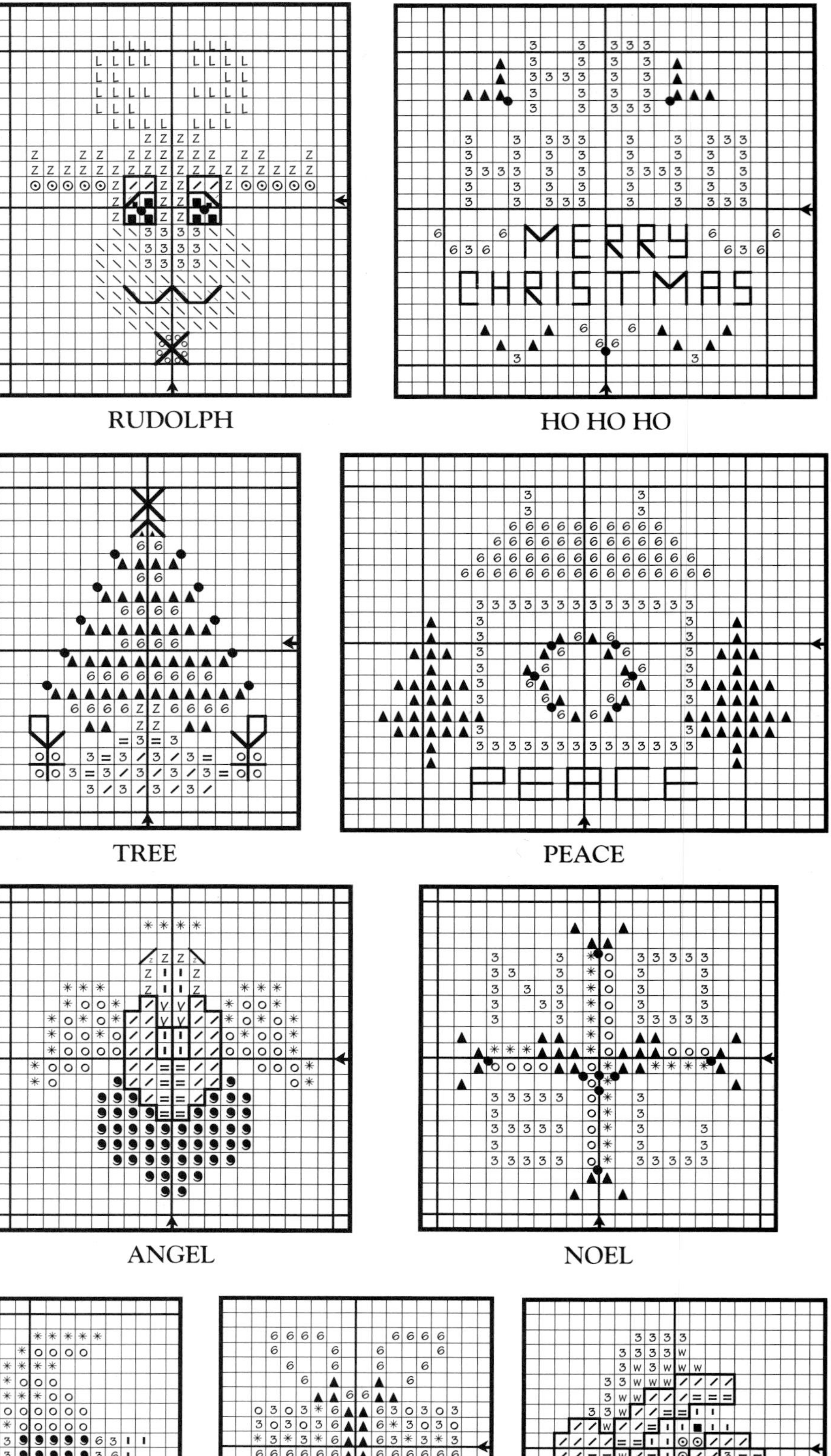

RUDOLPH

HO HO HO

TREE

PEACE

ANGEL

NOEL

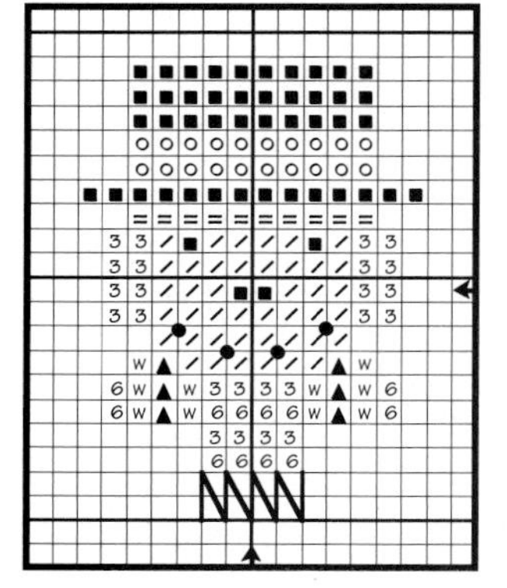

SNOWMAN

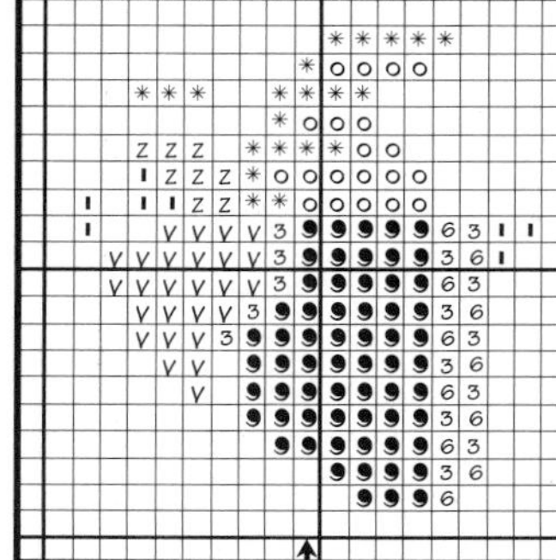

ANGEL SILHOUETTE

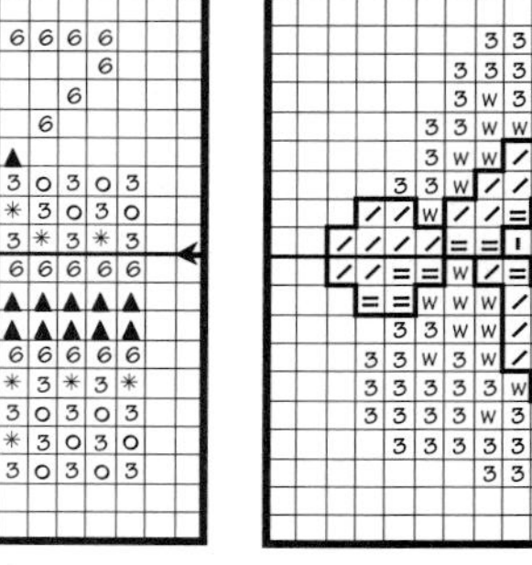

PACKAGE

SANTA

Gold Flower and Snowflake

These ornament designs take on an elegant appearance when popped into gold frames. The backstitching gives the illusion of a lot of work, but the time spent will be minimal. Unless you choose to reveal your secret, you'll be the only one who knows just how little effort was required to complete these pieces.

	DMC	COLOR
•	Metallic Gold	gold

Fabric: 14-count navy Aida from Charles Craft, Inc.

Stitch count:

Gold Flower	30H x 30W
Gold Snowflake	28H x 28W

Design size:

14-count

Gold Flower	2⅛" x 2⅛"
Gold Snowflake	2" x 2"

Instructions: Cross stitch using one strand Metallic Gold embroidery thread. Backstitch using one strand Metallic Gold embroidery thread.

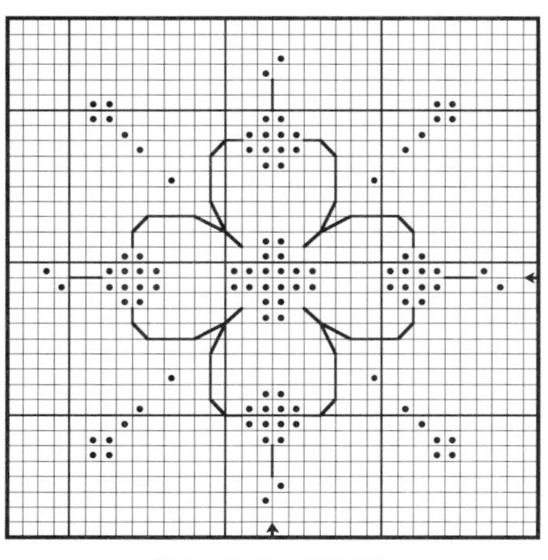

GOLD FLOWER

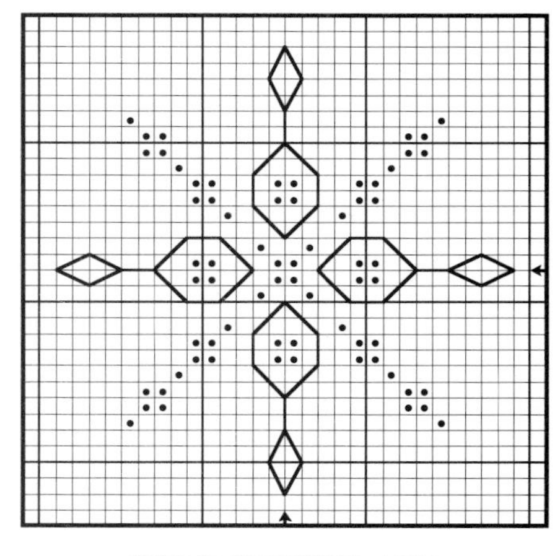

GOLD SNOWFLAKE

Frolicking Snowmen

What could be more charming than a family of little snowmen sending seasonal greetings from the band of a cross-stitch towel? These merry characters seem to have personalities all their own, and they'll be ideal for working alone or in pairs when time with needle and floss is limited. Work these adorable snow fellows on a sweatshirt and change a basic top into a holiday wearable that's sure to win compliments!

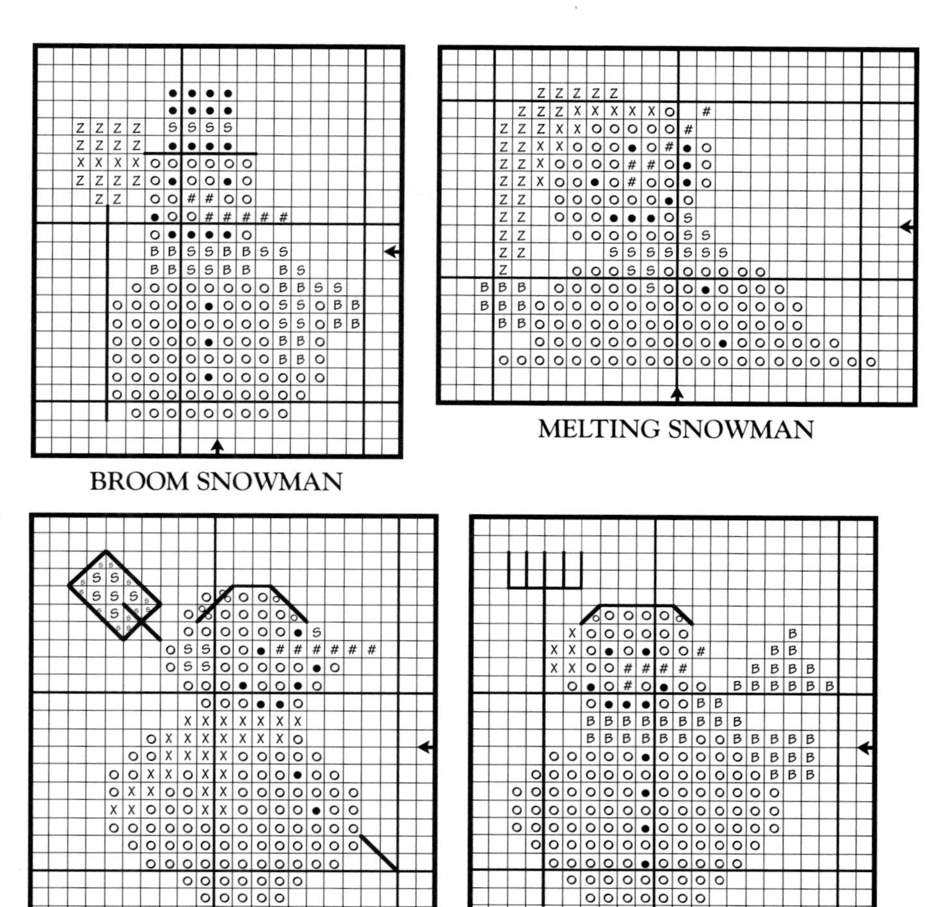

BROOM SNOWMAN

MELTING SNOWMAN

SHOVEL SNOWMAN

RAKE SNOWMAN

	DMC	COLOR
Z	745	yellow, lt. pl.
X	3687	mauve
O	white	white
•	814	garnet, dk.
B	3713	salmon, vy. lt.
#	834	olive, vy. lt.
S	3354	dusty rose, lt.

Fabric: 14-count antique blue Estate Towel from Charles Craft, Inc.

Stitch count:

Broom Snowman	19H x 16W
Melting Snowman	16H x 22W
Shovel Snowman	20H x 18W
Rake Snowman	20H x 18W
Tall Snowman	24H x 15W

Design size:

14-count

Broom Snowman	1⅜" x 1⅛"
Melting Snowman	1⅛" x 1⅝"
Shovel Snowman	1½" x 1¼"
Rake Snowman	1½" x 1¼"
Tall Snowman	1¾" x 1⅛"

Instructions: Cross stitch using four strands of floss. Backstitch using three strands 814. Center *Shovel Snowman* on cross-stitch fabric panel on towel. Stitch remaining designs on either side of *Shovel Snowman*, leaving sixteen squares between each and referring to photo for placement.

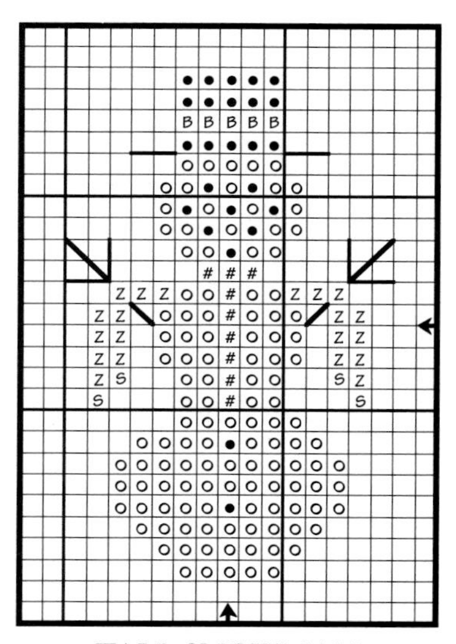

TALL SNOWMAN

Special Remembrances

Mark the holidays in stitches with this assortment of plant spikes. Include the *Happy Holiday* spike with a poinsettia to form a noteworthy present. The flowers you send Mom on Mothers' Day will be extra nice when they're arranged with a plant spike that conveys a message of love. Do you know someone who is housebound? Brighten her day with a basket of blooms and your favorite spike!

EASTER PLANT SPIKES

	DMC	COLOR
O	996	electric blue, med.
Z	554	violet, lt.
P	605	cranberry, vy. lt.
–	726	topaz, lt.
X	422	hazelnut, lt.
ℓ	828	blue, ul. lt.
З	703	chartreuse
bs	310	black

Fabric: 14-count white Aida

Stitch count: 26H x 24W
Design size:
14-count 1⅞" x 1¾"

Instructions: Cross stitch using three strands of floss. Backstitch using one strand of floss. Make straight stitches for blades of grass using one strand 703. Finishing instructions are on page 143.

Backstitch (bs) instructions:
703 grass
996 birds, *HAPPY EASTER*
310 remainder of backstitching

(Charts are on page 130.)

SPECIAL REMEMBRANCES PLANT SPIKES

	DMC	COLOR
⁖	676	old gold, lt.
//	783	gold
V	725	topaz
/	727	topaz, vy. lt.
3	321	red
X	347	salmon, dk.
C	3328	salmon, med.
II	760	salmon
O	740	tangerine
⊙	722	spice, lt.
▲	700	green, bt.
♡	469	avocado
★	562	jade, med.
U	564	jade, vy. lt.
6	797	royal blue
e	931	antique blue, med.
=	932	antique blue, lt.
a	340	blue-violet, med.
W	433	brown, med.
–	white	white

Fabric: 14-count white Aida
Stitch count: 16H x 22W
Design size:
14-count 1⅛" x 1⅝"

Instructions: Cross stitch using two strands of floss. Backstitch using one strand of floss unless otherwise indicated. Backstitch all lettering using two strands of floss. Make French knots where ● appears in *Happy Holidays* using three strands 321, wrapping floss around needle once.

Backstitch instructions:

469	stems in *With Love*, stems in *With Love For Mom*
347	*With Love*
321	heart in *God Bless*, all backstitching **except** star in *Happy Holiday*
783	star in *Happy Holiday*
700	stems in *Good Luck*
3328	heart in *With Love For Mom*, all backstitching in *Happy Easter*
931	lettering in *With Love For Mom*
740	lettering in *Good Luck*

Finishing instructions are on page 143.

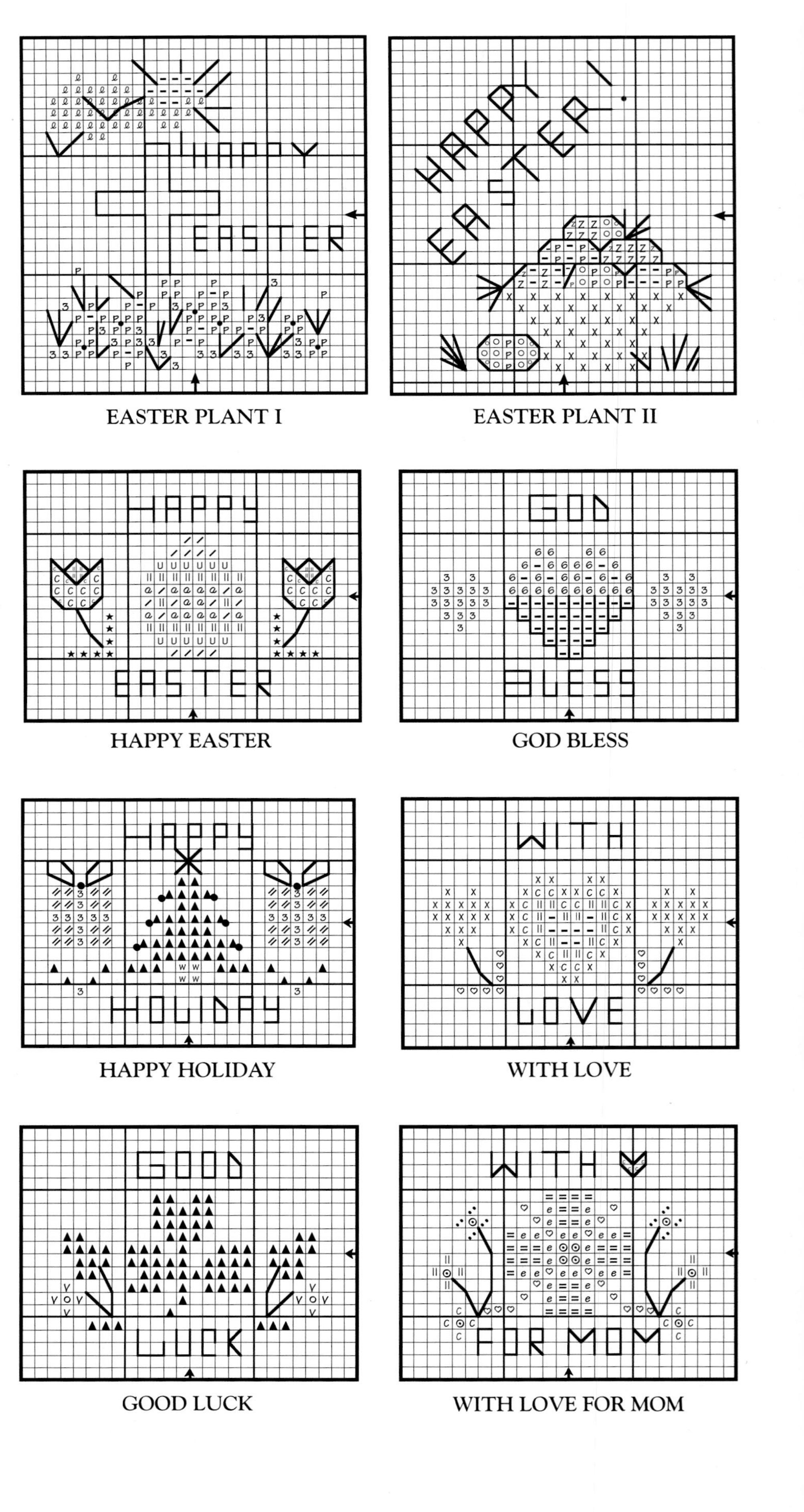

EASTER PLANT I

EASTER PLANT II

HAPPY EASTER

GOD BLESS

HAPPY HOLIDAY

WITH LOVE

GOOD LUCK

WITH LOVE FOR MOM

I Love You

The words "I love you" can never be said too often, and the feelings they convey linger long after being spoken. Stitch a reminder of your fondness for your Valentine on a colorful jar topper, and fill the jar with sweet treats for your darling.

	DMC	COLOR
3	321	red
X	469	avocado

Fabric: 25-count white Lugana® from Zweigart®
Stitch count: 12H x 12W
Design size:
25-count 1⅞" x 1⅞"

Instructions: Cross stitch over four threads using four strands of floss. Backstitch using four strands of floss.
Backstitch instructions:
469 leaves, stems
321 remainder of backstitching

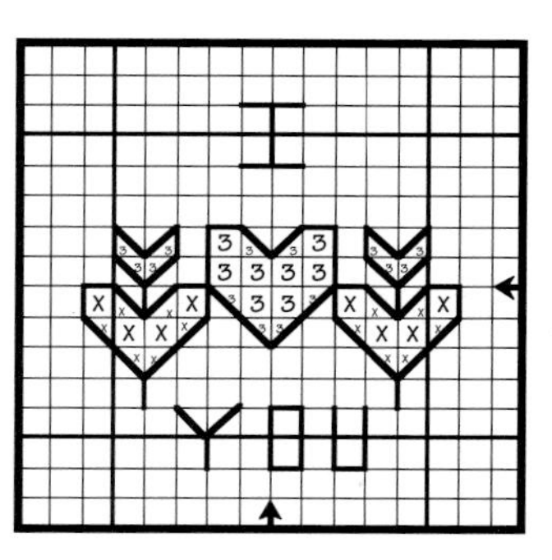

Christmas Jar Lids

Empty jars become notable containers when they're topped with stitched lids and filled with delicious goodies. Each of these designs is easy to complete and requires only a few shades of floss. Fill the jars with candy, cookies, hot chocolate powder, or a tasty spiced-tea mix, and you'll have quick-to-complete gifts the lucky recipients are sure to appreciate.

	DMC	COLOR
•	3362	pine green, dk.
R	817	coral red, vy. dk.
Y	725	topaz
O	white	white
B	797	royal blue
X	680	old gold, dk.
bs	310	black

Fabric: 25-count moss green Lugana® from Zweigart®
Stitch count: 24H x 20W
Design size:
25-count 2" x 1⅝"

Instructions: Cross stitch over two threads using two strands of floss. Backstitch using one strand of floss.
Backstitch instructions:
310 lettering, candlewick
817 candle flame

LET HEAVEN AND NATURE SING

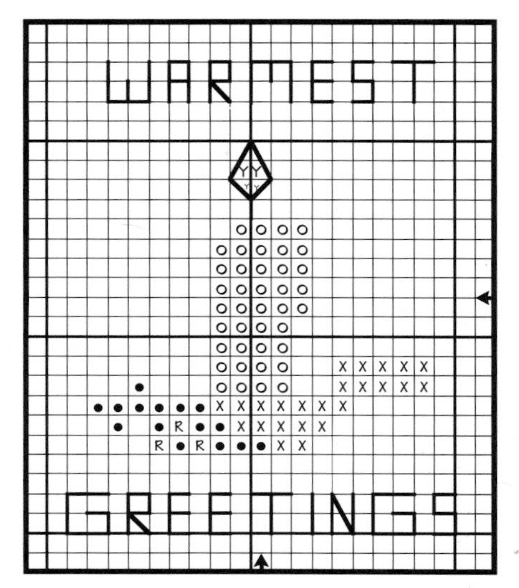

WARMEST GREETINGS

SEASONS GREETINGS

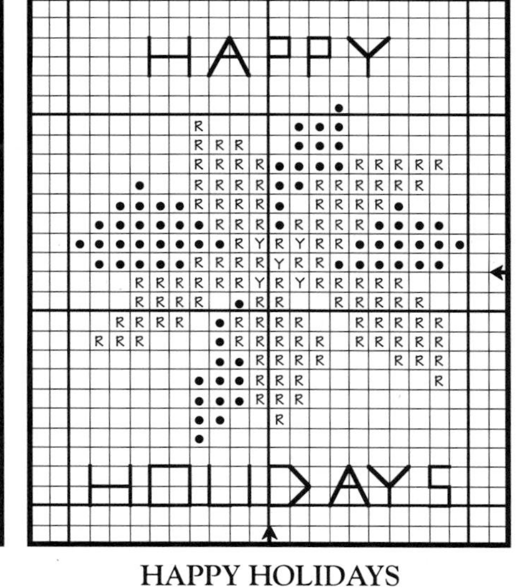

HAPPY HOLIDAYS

LET HEAVEN
AND NATURE
SING
WARMEST
GREETINGS
SEASONS
GREETINGS

Autumn Favorites

When the first chilly winds begin to blow and the leaves are transformed into a riot of fall colors, our thoughts turn to the autumn holidays. These designs capture the oranges and golds of the season. Finished as pins (far right), they'll allow you to welcome harvest-time in unique style. Fashion the top half of a frightfully cute outfit for your youngster by using a black turtleneck and your ingenuity! Be sure to choose a top that's machine washable—your trickster will want to wear it to school often during October. The tiny pumpkin will delight trick-or-treaters when stitched on a matching goodie bag.

JACK-O'-LANTERN AND PUMPKINS

	DMC	COLOR
B	975	gold-brown, dk.
X	970	pumpkin, lt.
•	704	chartreuse, bt.

Fabrics: ***Turtleneck***—20-count linen used as waste canvas on black turtleneck; ***Tote***—14-count black Aida tote from The JanLynn® Corporation

Stitch count:

Jack-o'-lantern	20H x 24W
Pumpkins	18H x 46H

Design size:

Jack-o'-lantern	20-count	2" x 2½"
	14-count	1½" x 1¾"
Pumpkins	20-count	1⅞" x 4⅝"

Turtleneck

Instructions: Cross stitch over two threads using four strands of floss. Backstitch using two strands 704. Stitch *Jack-o'-lantern* ¾" down from shoulder seam and 1" in from right-sleeve seam. Stitch *Pumpkins* ¾" in from left-side seam and 1½" above lower edge of shirt.

Tote

Instructions: Cross stitch using three strands of floss. Backstitch using two strands 704. Center *Jack-o'-lantern* 1½" below upper edge of tote. Repeat design on either side of middle design, leaving five squares between designs.

BOO AND HAPPY TURKEY

	DMC	COLOR
⋰	676	old gold, lt.
//	783	gold
V	725	topaz
O	740	tangerine
♡	469	avocado
●	400	mahogany, dk.
■	310	black
–	white	white
N	3776	mahogany, lt.

Fabric: 14-count white Aida
Stitch count: 16H x 22W
Design size:
14-count 1⅛" x 1⅝"

Instructions: Cross stitch using two strands of floss. Backstitch using one strand of floss unless otherwise indicated. Backstitch all lettering using two strands of floss. Make French knots where • appears at intersecting grid lines using two strands of floss, wrapping floss around needle once.

Backstitch instructions:

310	all backstitching in *Boo*, turkey in *Happy Turkey*
3776	corn in *Happy Turkey*
400	lettering in *Happy Turkey*

HAPPY THANKSGIVING

	DMC	COLOR
R	347	salmon, dk.
O	900	burnt orange, dk.
bs	400	mahogany, dk.
bs	783	gold

Fabric: 14-count oatmeal Rustico® Aida from Zweigart®
Stitch count: 26H x 32W
Design size:
14-count 1⅞" x 2¼"

Instructions: Cross stitch using two strands of floss. Backstitch using two strands of floss.

Backstitch (bs) instructions:

400	pumpkin stems and sections
783	wheat stalks

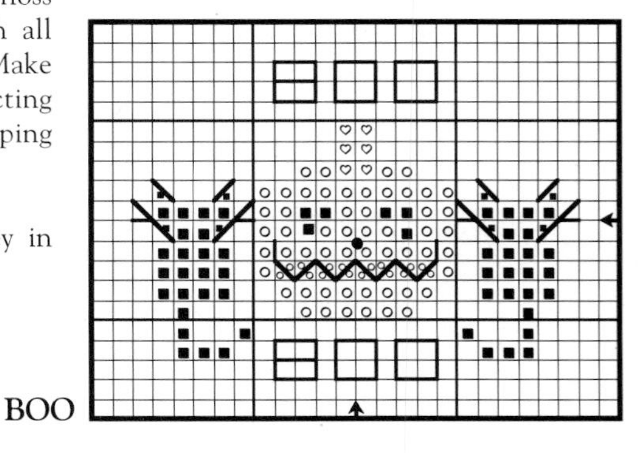

BOO

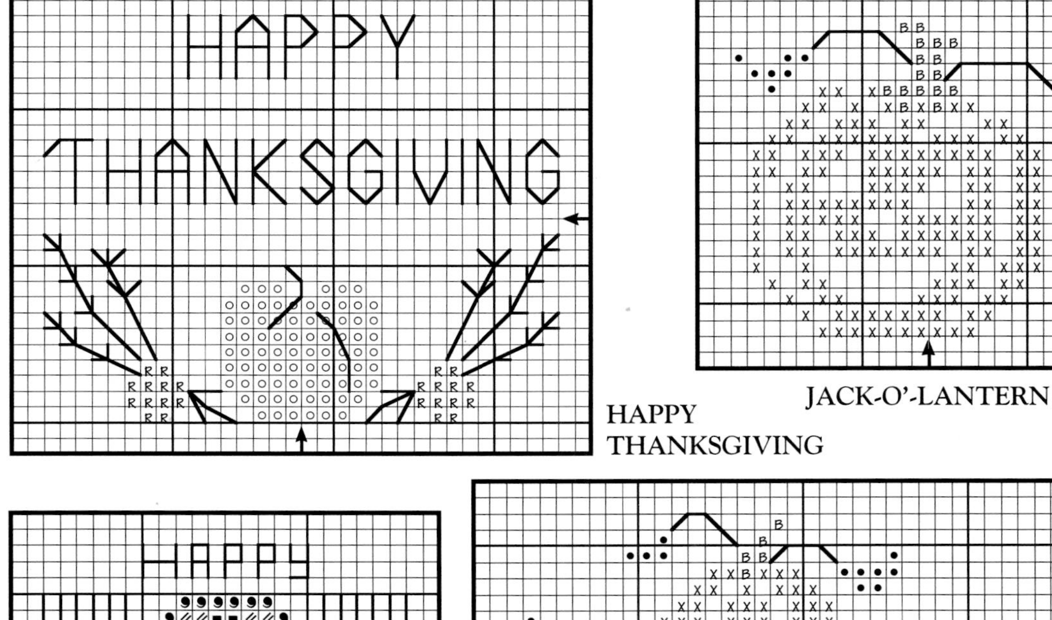

HAPPY THANKSGIVING

JACK-O'-LANTERN

To make pins, follow finishing instructions for *Butterflies* Hair Bow on page 142, omitting step 5, and glue pin back to center back of stiffened cross-stitch design.

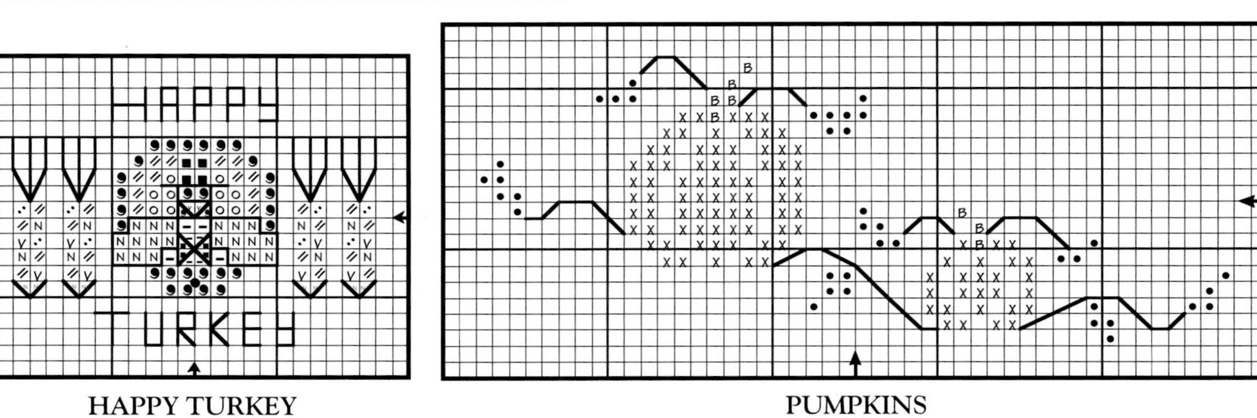

HAPPY TURKEY

PUMPKINS

Christmas Miniatures

Miniature Christmas pieces are great for making ahead and tucking away for last-minute giving needs. A pair of sachets, complete with cross stitch and filled with fragrant potpourri, make splendid quick gifts. Tiny stockings wearing the *Holly and Poinsettia* designs are the right size to hold small candy canes. Hang them on the tree or use them on wrapped packages for a personal touch.

NOEL

	DMC	COLOR
/	white	white
•	498	red, dk.
V	501	blue-green, dk.
3	500	blue-green, vy. dk.
bs	414	steel gray, dk.

Fabric: 14-count white Aida panel on sachet from Heart Strings
Stitch count: 14H x 22W
Design size:
14-count 1" x 1⅝"

Instructions: Cross stitch using two strands of floss. Backstitch (bs) using one strand 414. Center design on cross-stitch fabric panel of sachet.

STRAWBERRY

	DMC	COLOR
•	700	green, bt.
6	702	kelly green
X	817	coral red, vy. dk.
O	349	coral, dk.
/	352	coral, lt.
C	725	topaz
=	white	white
bs	414	steel gray, dk.

Fabric: 14-count white Aida panel on sachet from Heart Strings
Stitch count: 15H x 19W
Design size:
14-count 1⅛" x 1⅜"

Instructions: Cross stitch using two strands of floss. Backstitch (bs) using one strand 414. Center design on cross-stitch fabric panel of sachet.

HOLLY AND POINSETTIA

	DMC	COLOR
•	321	red
X	699	green
M	Metallic Gold	gold

Fabric: 14-count ivory Aida panel on Mini Stockings from Charles Craft, Inc.
Stitch count:
Poinsettia 15H x 18W
Holly 19H x 16W
Design size:
14-count
Poinsettia 1⅛" x 1¼"
Holly 1⅜" x 1⅛"

Instructions: Cross stitch using three strands of floss. Cross stitch using two strands Metallic Gold embroidery thread. Center design on cross-stitch fabric panel of stocking.

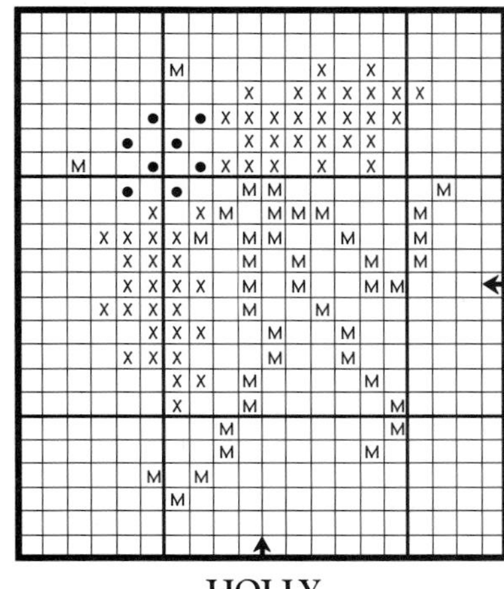

HOLLY

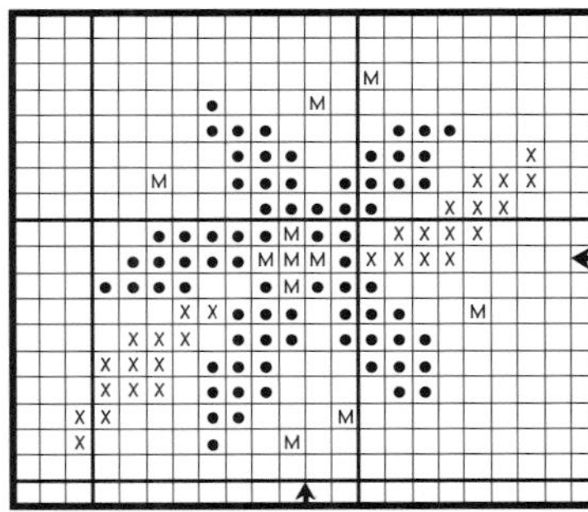

POINSETTIA

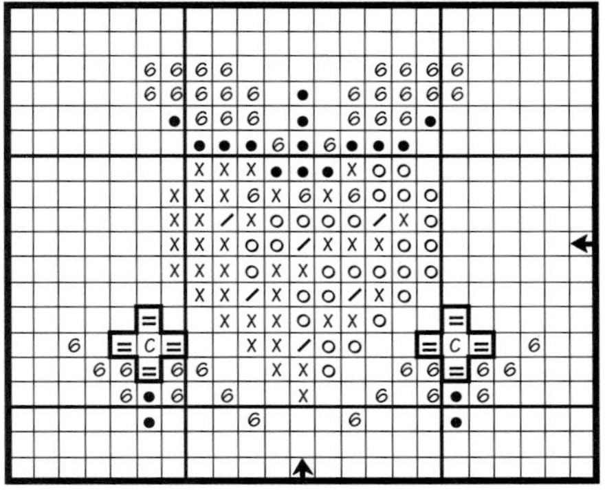

STRAWBERRY

NOEL

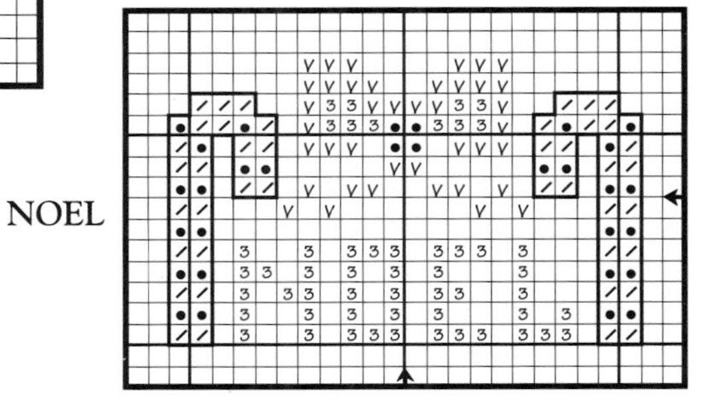

(Sachets available from The Cross Stitch Shoppe, 2116 Old Montgomery Highway, Pelham, AL 35124, (205)733-1682.)

Holly Alphabet

This festive *Holly Alphabet* opens up endless possibilities for stitching and giving. The letters, shown here on the band of a cross-stitch towel and also finished as the *Peace Bellpull*, provide hours of needlework pleasure. A single letter will make an attractive ornament when centered in a plastic frame. These yuletide letters can also be combined to spell the family name. When matted and framed, your completed stitchery will become a treasured seasonal piece. To set an unforgettable table, work each family member's name on a place mat and stitch their first initials on matching napkins. Let your imagination take over!

PEACE BELLPULL

	DMC	COLOR
■	319	pistachio, vy. dk.
X	321	red

Fabric: 20-count natural Irish linen from Charles Craft, Inc.
Stitch count: 88H x 16W
Design size:
20-count 8⅞" x 1⅝"

Instructions: Cross stitch over two threads using four strands of floss. Backstitch date and tree trunk using two strands 319. Make straight stitches for tree limbs using two strands 319. Make French knots where • appears at intersecting grid lines using three strands 321, wrapping floss around needle once. Finishing instructions are on page 142.

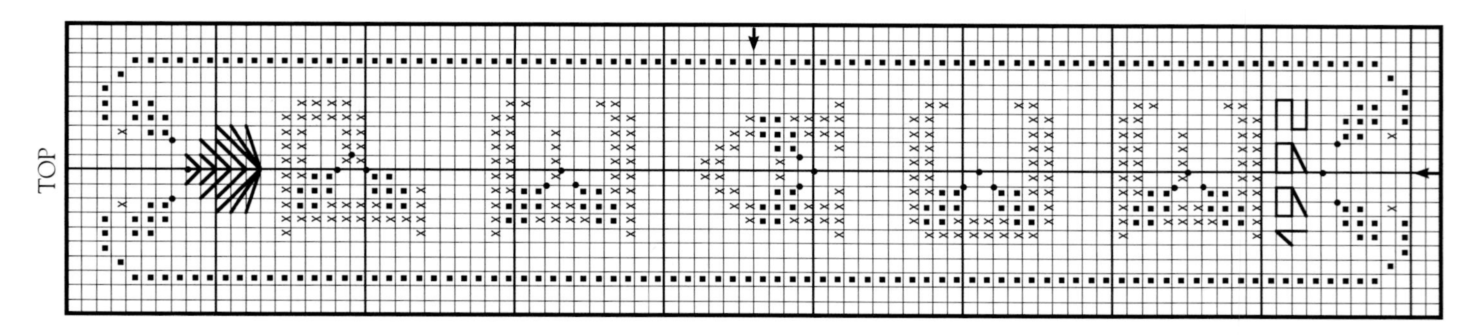

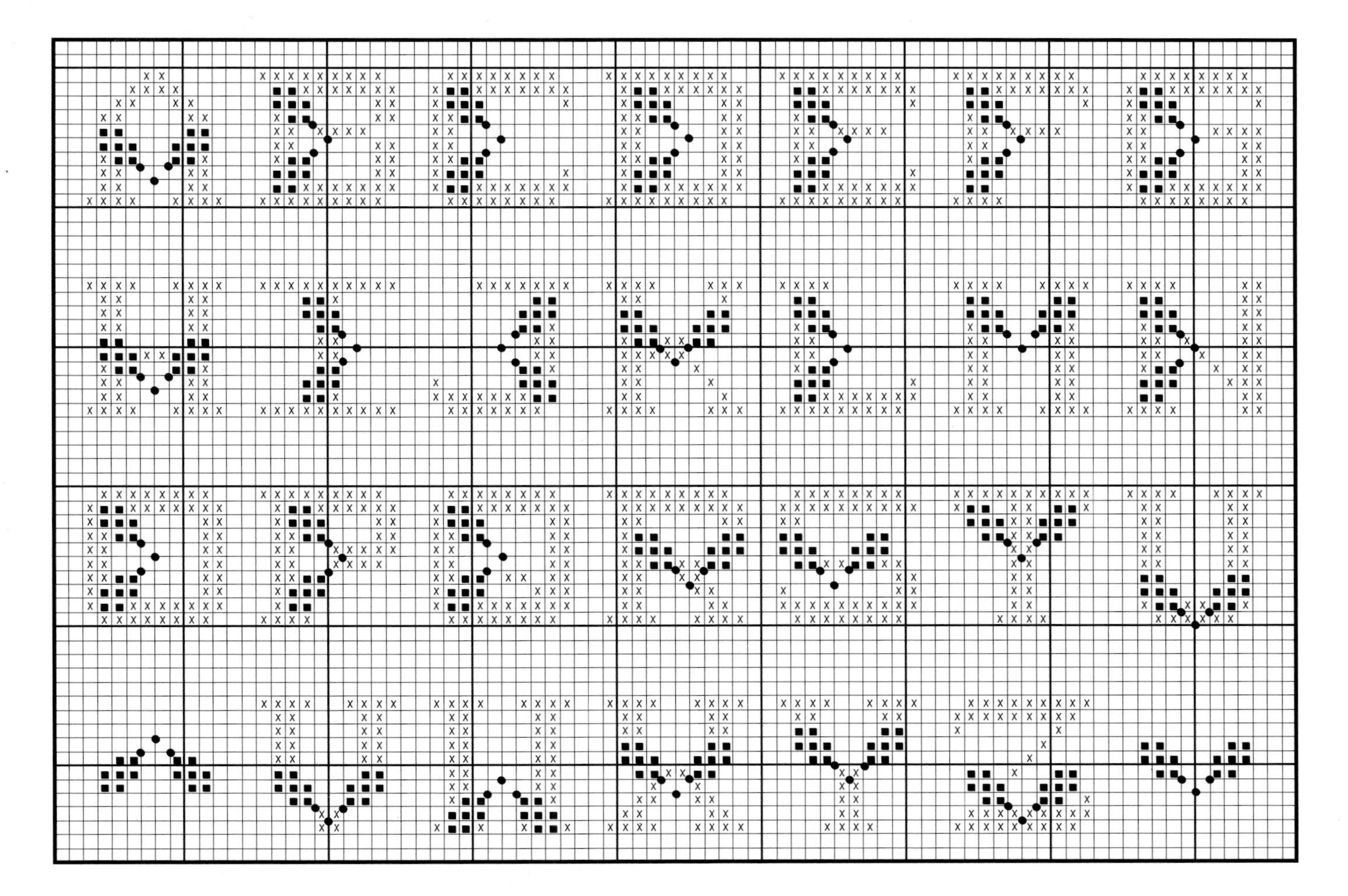

HOLLY ALPHABET

	DMC	COLOR
■	319	pistachio, vy. dk.
X	321	red

Fabric: 14-count yellow Park Avenue Fingertips™ towel from Charles Craft, Inc.

Stitch count:

Letters	10H x 10W
Holly Motif	4H x 8W

Design size:

Letters	¾" x ¾"
Holly Motif	¼" x ⅝"

Instructions: Cross stitch using two strands of floss. Make French knots where ● appears at intersecting grid lines using three strands 321, wrapping floss around needle once. Center lettering on cross-stitch fabric panel on towel, leaving two squares between each letter. When lettering is complete, center *Holly Motif* for upper and lower border. Repeat designs to edges of towel, leaving two squares between each.

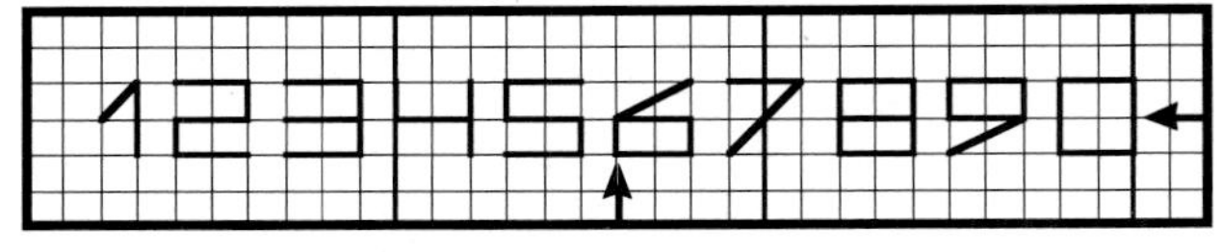

PEACE BELLPULL NUMERALS

General Instructions for Cross Stitch

Basic Supplies: Even-weave fabric, tapestry needle(s), six-strand embroidery floss, embroidery scissors, embroidery hoop (optional).

Fabric Preparation: Determine size of fabric needed for a project by dividing number of horizontal stitches by thread count of fabric. For example, if a design 35-stitches wide is worked on 14-count fabric, it will cover 2½" (35 divided by 14 equals 2½). Repeat process for vertical count. Add three inches on all sides of design area to find dimensions for cutting fabric. Whipstitch edges to prevent fraying.

Floss Preparation: Cut floss into 14" to 18" lengths. Separate all six strands. Reunite number of strands needed and thread needle, leaving one floss end longer than the other.

Where to Start: Start wherever you like. Some designers suggest finding center of fabric and starting there. Others recommend beginning with a central motif, while still others work borders first. Many find fabric center, count up and back to the left, and start with the uppermost-left stitch. Wherever you begin, be sure to leave allowance for all horizontal and vertical stitches so that a 3" fabric margin is left around completed design.

Should you choose to begin at the center point, find it by folding fabric from top to bottom and then from left to right. Use a straight pin to mark upper-left corner at junction of folds, and then unfold fabric. Pin will be in center of fabric.

Many of the projects included in this book feature a single motif or several related motifs stitched together to form a design. When a single motif is used, center the motif in the area to be stitched unless stitching instructions give specific placement instructions. When several motifs that have been charted separately are combined to form a larger design, follow placement instructions given in the stitching instructions for the project.

After deciding where to begin on fabric, find same point on graph. Each square on graph represents one stitch. Those squares containing a symbol (i.e., X,T,O) indicate that a stitch should be made in that space over those threads. Different symbols represent different colors of floss for stitches. (See color code of chart.) They may also indicate partial or decorative stitches. Familiarize yourself with color code before you begin stitching. Even-weave fabric may be stretched over an embroidery hoop to facilitate stitching.

Stitching the Design: Using the illustrations on page 141, stitch design, completing all full and partial cross stitches first. Cross all full cross stitches in same direction to achieve a smooth surface appearance. Work backstitches second and any decorative stitches last.

Helpful Hints for Stitching: Do not knot floss. Instead, catch end on back of work with first few stitches. As you stitch, pull floss through fabric "holes" with one stroke, not several short ones. The moment you feel resistance from floss, cease pulling. Consistent tension on floss results in a smoother look for stitches. Drop your needle frequently to allow floss to untwist. It twists naturally as you stitch and, as it gets shorter, must be allowed to untwist more often. To begin a new color on project, prepare floss and secure new strands as noted. To end stitching, run floss under several completed stitches on the back and clip remaining strands close to surface. Many times it is necessary to skip a few spaces (threads) on the fabric in order to continue a row of stitches in the same color. If you must skip an area covering more than ¼", end stitching as described above and begin again at next point. This procedure prevents uneven tension on the embroidery surface and snagging on back. It also keeps colors from showing through unstitched areas. Do not carry thread over an area that will remain unstitched.

When You Are Finished: For designs using cotton or linen floss on cotton or linen even-weave fabric, hand wash piece with mild detergent in warm water. Rinse thoroughly with cold water. Roll in terry towel and squeeze gently to remove excess moisture. Do not wring. Unroll towel and allow piece to dry until barely damp. Iron on padded surface with design face down, using medium setting for heat. A press cloth will help prevent shine on dark fabrics. **Note:** Acrylics, acrylic blends, wools, or silks must be treated differently when cleaning. Check manufacturer's guidelines for special cleaning instructions.

Helpful Hints for Cross Stitch: The instructions and yardage for finishing materials have been written and calculated for each of the projects shown, stitched on the fabric listed in each color code. If you wish to stitch a design on an alternate fabric or alter its placement, you will need to recalculate the finished size of the project, as well as the yardage of finishing materials needed, and make the necessary dimension adjustments when purchasing supplies and making the projects.

Stitching with Waste Canvas or Linen: Determine the size piece of waste canvas or linen you will need for a project by referring to the stitch count and design size of the design to be used. Cut the waste canvas or linen accordingly, allowing at least a 2" margin around perimeter of design. Baste waste canvas or linen securely in place on garment to prevent garment from stretching while you stitch. If garment is stretched during stitching, cross stitches will be distorted when waste canvas or linen is removed. Stitch through the waste canvas or linen and the garment underneath. When you have completed the stitching, remove the waste canvas by wetting the area and gently pulling each strand individually. Remove linen by gently pulling each strand individually. It is not necessary to wet the linen before removing the strands. Remove basting threads.

Notes about Stitching on Purchased Items: With the wonderful fabrics available today, finding high-quality, ready-to-wear garments and accessories suitable for embellishing with cross stitch is easy. Cotton garments are easier to stitch on and care for than most synthetics. Cottons and cotton knits are great for babies.

Securing the floss on the back of your work is very important, particularly when stitching is done on garments and accessories that will be washed and dried. Leave extra-long floss tails while stitching and weave them through many stitches on the back before clipping.

Be sure to wash and dry any washable piece you plan to stitch on prior to stitching. This will help prevent distortion of stitching should the item shrink. Pieces that bleed when washed should be soaked in a solution of one part vinegar to eight parts water to set the colors. Rinse and wash again following manufacturer's instructions on label. To prevent floss colors from bleeding onto washable garments, bleed floss in a solution of one part vinegar to eight parts water prior to stitching. Soak floss one skein at a time and rinse thoroughly until water remains clear, repeating for each skein. Lay floss flat on a towel to dry, being careful not to tangle floss.

Linen scraps were used in place of waste canvas for stitching on many of the ready-made pieces featured throughout this book. Using linen in place of waste canvas allows you to work decorative stitches in areas where waste canvas is too bulky to work with. In addition, when linen is used, your stitches will be more evenly spaced and consistent and will lie closer to the fabric.

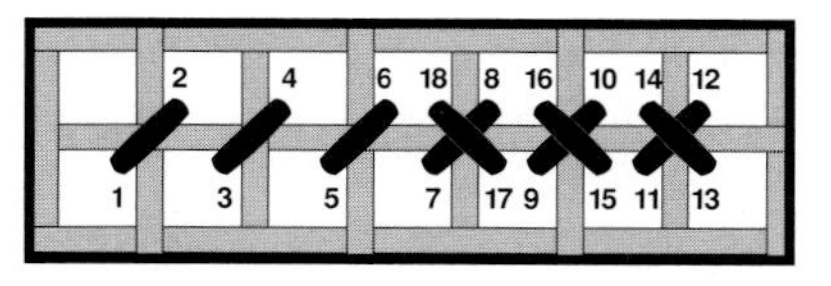

Full Cross Stitch (over one thread)

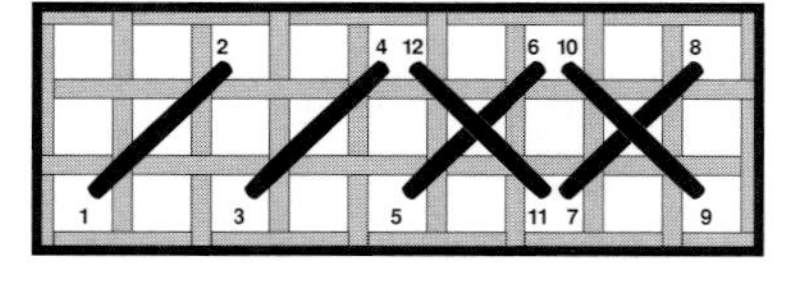

Full Cross Stitch (over two threads)

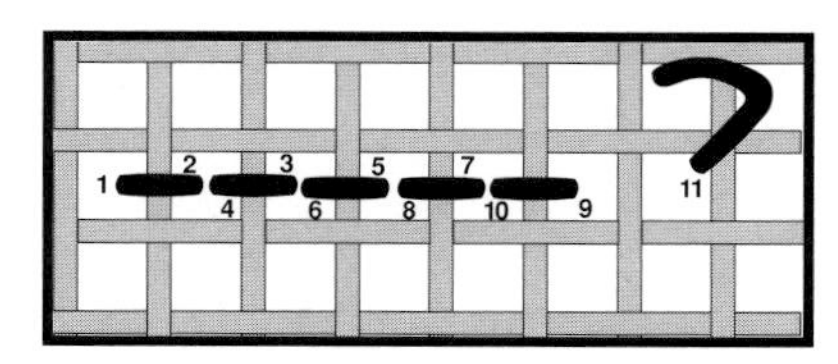

Basic Backstitch

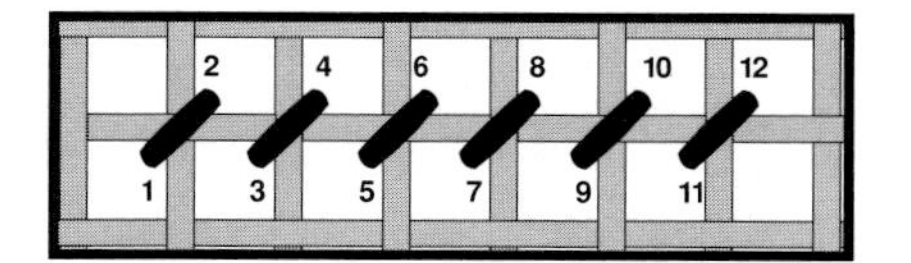

Basic ½ Cross Stitch (over one thread)

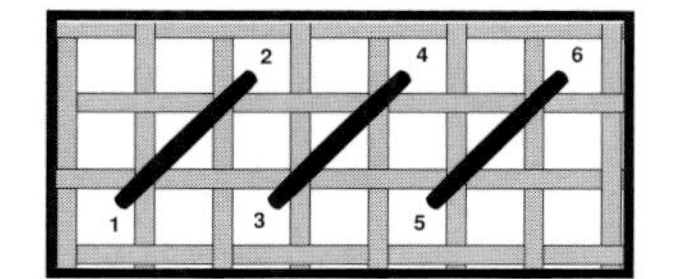

½ Cross Stitch (over two threads)

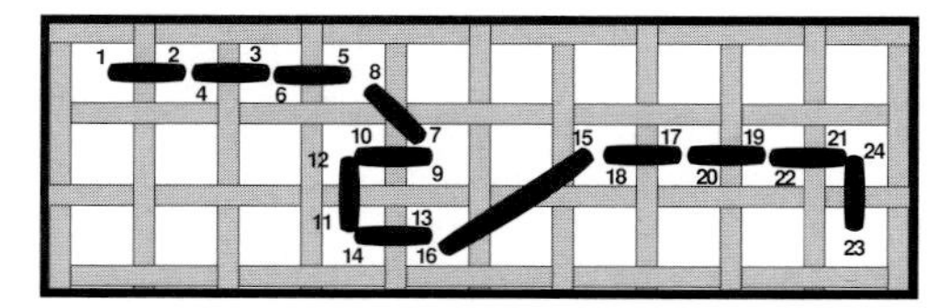

Backstitch (showing variations)

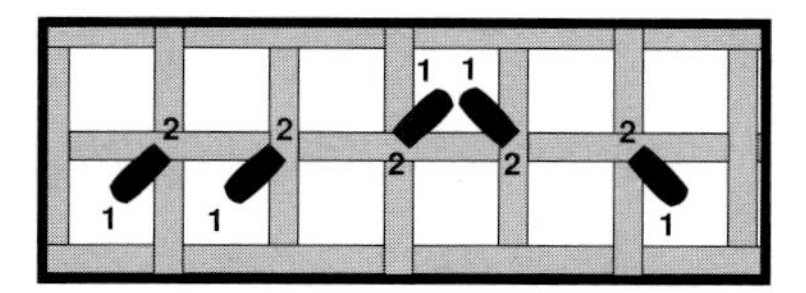

¼ Cross Stitch (over one thread)

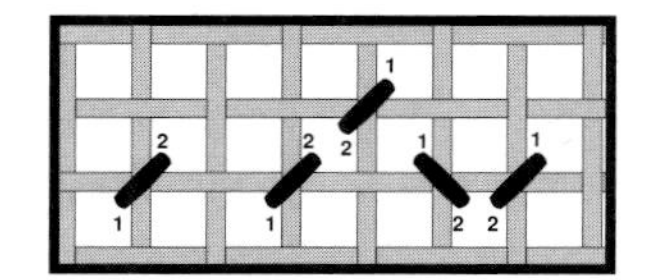

¼ Cross Stitch (over two threads)

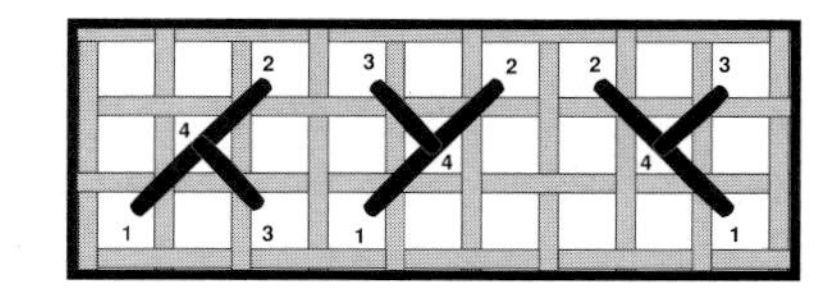

¾ Cross Stitch (over two threads)

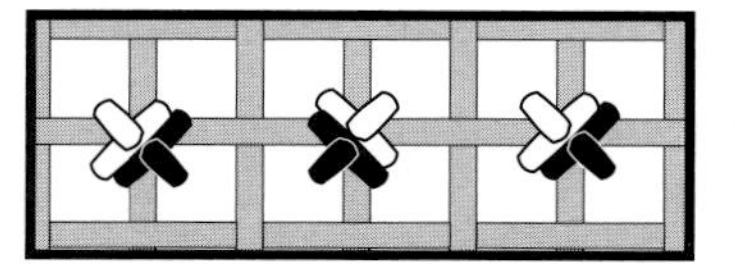

Two ¾ Stitches (in one square, using two different floss colors)

¾ Cross Stitches (over one in various positions)

Backstitch (across two ¾ stitches and around full cross)

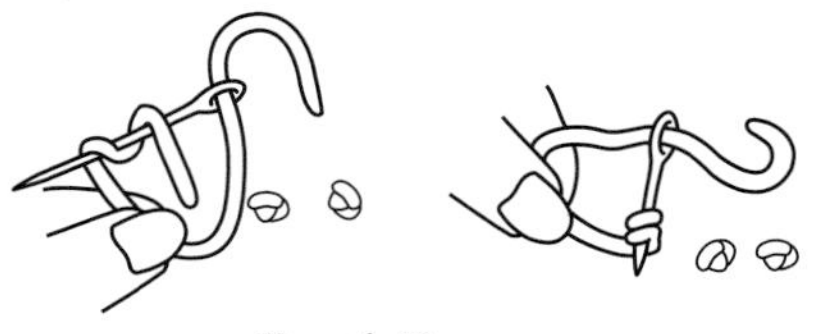

French Knot

Finishing Instructions

Butterflies Hair Bows

Materials:
Purchased hair bows   Waxed paper
Aleene's Fabric Stiffener **or** fresh white glue and water
Press cloth   Iron
Sharp scissors   Hot glue gun

1. Complete cross stitch following instructions given.
2. To stiffen, saturate entire piece of fabric in fabric stiffener or a one-to-one solution of fresh white glue and water. Gently squeeze out excess. Lay flat on waxed paper to dry. Let dry thoroughly.
3. When fabric is completely dry, press from wrong side as needed to smooth, using a press cloth.
4. Cut cross-stitch fabric around perimeter of stitched design, following outline of design as a guide for cutting, staying at least one space away from stitched design, being careful not to cut working threads.
5. Glue stiffened butterflies to purchased hair bows.

Peace Bellpull

Materials:
3¼" x 12" piece muslin (for backing)
Medium-weight interfacing
3"-wide brass bellpull hardware
Hand-sewing needle
Scissors   Straight pins
Sewing machine   Iron

1. Complete cross stitch following instructions given.
2. Sew basting stitches along sides of stitched front to fit width of hardware, centering design between basting lines. Trim cross-stitch fabric to 3¼" x 12".
3. Place stitched front and backing fabric with right sides together, aligning edges. Sew long edges together, using a ½" seam allowance. Turn right-side out and press.
4. Run excess fabric at top of design through top piece of bellpull hardware and fold fabric to back side, leaving ⅜" on front between top of stitched design and fold. Turn raw edges of fabric under and hand-stitch to backing fabric. Repeat at bottom of bellpull.

Pinwheel Bouquet Bow

Materials:
Hand-sewing needle
Small basket   Ecru thread
Scissors   Hot glue gun

1. Complete cross stitch following instructions given.
2. To form bow, lay 7½" Ribband® strip right-side down on a flat surface. Fold ends of strip to center, overlap, and baste together. To form center of bow, center flower motif stitched on 2¾" Ribband® strip over center front of bow. Fold ends of strip to back around center area of bow and overlap ends. Adjust bow and bow center, baste ends of bow center together, and tack bow and bow center together at center back with blind stitches.
3. Glue bow to basket.

Tulips and Hearts Mug Coaster

Materials:
5"-square piece cross-stitch fabric (for backing)
Thread to match
Polyester filling **or** 4¾"-square lightweight batting
Scissors   Sewing machine

1. Complete cross stitch following instructions given.
2. Trim fabric, leaving a 1" margin on all sides.
3. Place stitched front and backing with wrong sides together, centering a thin layer of polyester filling or batting between fabric pieces and aligning fabric edges. Machine stitch around perimeter of stitched design ½" away from edge.
4. Fringe by pulling threads from fabric edges to machine stitching.

Pillows—
Back Door Welcome
Counting Sheep
Pineapple Monogram
Thistle
Tooth Fairy
Welcome

Note: For these projects, a general materials list is given. Individual materials for each project are listed separately.

General materials:
Polyester filling   Straight pins
Scissors   Iron
Sewing machine with zipper foot
Hand-sewing needle
Thread to match backing fabrics

Back Door Welcome
Materials:
⅓ yd. 44/45"-wide complementary print fabric (for backing and ruffle)
¾ yd. ½"-wide red ribbon (for hanger and bow)

Counting Sheep
Materials:
4¼" x 5¼" scrap complementary fabric (for backing)
20" length 1"-wide white eyelet trim
7" length ¼"-wide white ribbon (for hanger)

Pineapple Monogram
Materials:
13"-square piece complementary fabric (for backing)
60" complementary purchased piping

Thistle
Materials:
⅝ yd. 44/45"-wide complementary print fabric (for backing and ruffle)

Tooth Fairy
Materials:
Two 6" x 4½" scraps white fabric (for pillow front and backing)
1 yd. purchased lavender piping
¾ yd. ¾"–1"-wide white lace trim

Welcome
Materials:
3¾" x 5" scrap complementary fabric (for backing)
½ yd. purchased red piping
7" length ⅛"-wide red ribbon (for hanger)

Back Door Welcome and *Thistle*:
1. Complete cross stitch following instructions given.
2. For *Back Door Welcome*, cut one 5¼" x 8½" piece from fabric for backing. Cut 2½"-wide strips from fabric and piece together to make at least 48" for ruffle. For *Thistle*, cut one 10" square from fabric for pillow backing. Cut 6½"-wide strips from fabric and piece together to make at least 80" for ruffle. Set aside.
3. Fold ruffle strip in half lengthwise and press. Sew a gathering thread along raw-edge side of strip ⅜" in from edge of fabric and another ¼" in from edge of fabric. Gather ruffle, placing around pillow and adjusting fullness as needed. Pin ruffle around perimeter of pillow front, aligning raw edge of ruffle with raw edge of pillow front. Sew ruffle to pillow front, using a ½" seam allowance and being careful not to catch ruffle.
4. Pin pillow front to pillow back with right sides together and sew around perimeter along stitching line, leaving an opening at bottom of pillow for turning. Trim seams, clip corners, and turn. Stuff with polyester filling. Blind stitch opening closed.
5. For *Back Door Welcome*, cut a 7" length of ribbon and tack ends to back of pillow at top corners. Tie a bow in remaining length of ribbon and tack center of bow at center of hanging ribbon.

Pineapple Monogram, Welcome, and *Counting Sheep*:
1. Complete cross stitch following instructions given.

2. Trim cross-stitch fabric to size of backing fabric for each pillow. Sew a stitching line ½" in from edges around perimeter of stitched front.
3. Place piping/eyelet trim around perimeter of stitched front with raw edge of piping/eyelet trim toward raw edge of cross-stitch fabric. Align stitching line on piping/eyelet trim with stitching line on stitched front and machine stitch piping/eyelet trim to pillow front, using zipper foot on machine for piping.
4. Pin pillow front to pillow back with right sides together and sew around perimeter along stitching line, leaving an opening at bottom of pillow for turning. Trim seams, clip corners, and turn. Stuff with polyester filling. Blind stitch opening closed.
5. For *Welcome* and *Counting Sheep*, tack ribbon ends to back of pillow close to top corners.

Tooth Fairy:
1. Complete cross stitch following instructions given.
2. Trim cross-stitch fabric to 6" x 4". Turn top edge under ¾". Press. Sew piping across top edge.
3. Place pillow front right-side up atop a flat surface. Place stitched front right-side up atop pillow front, aligning edges. Pin. Sew a stitching line around perimeter ½" in from raw edges, attaching pillow front and cross-stitched pocket together along sides and at bottom.
4. Place piping around perimeter of assembled pillow front with raw edge of piping toward raw edge of fabric. Align stitching line on piping with stitching line on pillow front and machine stitch piping to pillow front, using zipper foot on machine. Repeat for white lace trim.
5. Pin pillow front to pillow back with right sides together and sew around perimeter along stitching line, leaving an opening at bottom of pillow for turning. Trim seams, clip corners, and turn. Stuff with polyester filling. Blind stitch opening closed.

Plant Spikes—
Special Occasions
Special Remembrances
Welcome Baby

Materials:
Aleene's Fabric Stiffener **or** fresh white glue and water
Waxed paper
Press cloth
Iron
Sharp scissors
Plant spikes (available at floral shops and craft stores)
Hot glue gun **or** masking tape

1. Complete cross stitch following instructions given.
2. Follow instructions 2–3 for *Butterflies hair bows*.
3. Cut cross-stitch fabric around perimeter of stitched design, staying at least one space away from stitched design and being careful not to cut working threads.
4. Place blunt end of plant spike on wrong side of stitched front, centering spike. Glue or tape spike to back side of stitched design.

Designers

Charlotte Holder
Acorn and Leaf, 22
Apples for the Teacher, 108
Bug Alphabet, 48
Butterflies, 100
Circus Clowns, 9
Counting Sheep, 38
Dinosaurs, 26
Easter Plant I, 129
Easter Plant II, 129
Eat Dessert First, 76
Farm Animals, 9
Floral Alphabet, 45
Floral Border, 58
Flower Basket, 101
Frolicking Snowmen, 126
Happy Holidays, 132
Just for Cowboys, 43
Let Heaven and Nature Sing, 132
Mauve Flower, 101
Noah's Ark, 28
Sailboat and Anchor, 26
School Bus, 40
School Days, 13, 109
Sea Life, 8, 34
Seasons Greetings, 132
Soccer Ball, 40
Tooth Fairy, 37
Veggies, 72
Warmest Greetings, 132
Watermelons, 12, 109
Welcome, 88, 90

Cathy Livingston
ABC Blocks, 56
A Smile for You, 98
Back Door Welcome, 89
Bear With Balloons, 50
Bluebirds and Hearts, 117
Boo, 134
Bright Sunglasses, 35
Bunny "Tales", 52
Calico Rooster, 81
Coral Flowers, 113
Ducklings, 38
For Your New Home, 98
Fruit Stack Welcome, 89
Get Well, 98
God Bless, 128
Good Luck, 128
Happy Clown, 53
Happy Easter, 129
Happy Holiday, 128
Happy Turkey, 134
Holly Alphabet, 138
Holly Leaves, 23
Home Sweet Home, 92
I Love You, 131
Mini Fruits, 68
Mini Ornaments, 122
Miniature Houses, 62, 87
Neon Tricycle, 40
Noel, 136
Peace Bellpull, 138
Peach Flower, 101
Pear Tree, 71
Pineapple Monogram, 20, 84, 116
Sampler Motif, 93
Sewing Tools, 104
Southwestern Motif, 93
Strawberry, 136
Sunshine Fun, 26
Sweet Dreams, 38
Teatime, 103
Thistle, 84
Tulips and Hearts, 66
Welcome Baby, 119
White Florals Quartet, 114
With Love, 128
With Love for Mom, 128

Claudia Wood
At the Beach, 34
Ballet Slippers, 118
Bright Balloons, 50
Eat Smart, 76
Forget-me-not Bouquet, 15, 59
Gold Flower and Snowflake, 125
Happy 4th, 98
Happy Birthday, 98
Happy Thanksgiving, 134
Health Is True Wealth, 76
Hearts and Flowers, 96
Holly and Poinsettia, 136
Ivy Wreath and Swag, 110
Jack-o'-lantern and *Pumpkins*, 134
Make Me Beautiful, 107
Notable Quote, 91
One-color Floral, 115
Pinwheel Bouquet, 54
Posy Border, 44
Rainbow Alphabet, 30, 31
Red Chilies, 19, 79
Shoes, 104
Southwestern Stitchery, 78, 79
Sunflowers, 18
Tea Party, 65, 103
Thank You, 98
Vine Alphabet, 16, 112

Stitchers

Laura Boyd, Susan Branch, Susan Brothers, Kayla Connors, Cathy Cunningham, Kelly Davis, Shannon Griffin, Susan Hicks, Debbie Kendrick, Rebecca Langston, Tanya Matherne, Felicia McEachin, Emily Neel, Jeff Odom, Catherine Scott, Hilda Smith, April Taylor, Carrie Thibodeaux, Ginger Traywick, Cathy Watford, Kelley Zeanah, Tonda Zimmerman

Custom Finishing

Maureen Mayfield, Claudia Wood

Computer Charting

Susan Branch, Rebecca Mitchell, Robyn Taylor

Index

Numbers in **bold** type indicate color photo pages. Numbers in regular type indicate chart and color code pages.